Investment Clubs

HOW TO START AND RUN ONE
THE MOTLEY FOOL WAY

by Selena Maranjian

 The Motley Fool, Inc.

Published by The Motley Fool, Inc., 123 North Pitt Street,
Alexandria, Virginia, 22314, USA

First Printing, June 1998
10 9 8 7 6 5 4 3 2 1

ISBN 1-892547-00-7

Printed in the United States of America
Set in ITC Century Book

Acknowledgments

Few Foolish products are created by a single Fool and this primer is no exception. There are many people to thank and chief among them is David Forrest, who contributed significantly to the section on picking and evaluating companies. Other Fools who helped out on this project include editors Brian Bauer and Jennifer Silber, writers of fool.com source material Randy Befumo and Rick Aristotle Munarriz, legal beagle Lawrence Greenberg, project manager extraordinaire Ginger Huang, tax maven Roy Lewis, and production specialists Debora Tidwell and Mia Tidwell.

Providing much insight into the working of investment clubs were our many readers, who have been discussing club issues on our message boards. Some generous club members reviewed our work-in-progress, offering valuable feedback and suggestions. In addition, some clubs agreed to let us publish their minutes and agendas. Much thanks to the following individuals and clubs:

Pam Bomar and The Exchange Club and Boise Street Investment Club in Portland, Oregon

Dana Jenkins and the Hera Investment Group in Columbus, Ohio

Jane Smolens and the W.A.I.F. Investment Club and W.O.W. Investment Club of Palos Verdes, California

Angie Smyers and the Hera Investment Group in Columbus, Ohio

Joan Van Liew and the Common Cents Investment Club in Galesburg, Illinois

Contents

- The Pitfall of the Pernicious Co-Member
- The Danger of Under-Delegation
- The Entanglement of Ennui
- The Snare of Subterfuge
- The Booby Trap of Time
- The Menace of Math
- The Hazard of Humorlessness
- The Jeopardy of Jelly Donuts

General Foolish Investing
- What We Avoid
- What We Embrace
- A Bunch of Eggs, A Bunch of Baskets

Picking Stocks
- A Starting Point: Your Best Friend
- Gathering Information
- Digging Deeper

A Company's Price Tag
- The Price-to-Earnings (P/E) Ratio
- The Fool Ratio (PEG Ratio)
- The Price-to-Sales Ratio (PSR)

Keep in Touch!

A Glossary for Beginning Investors

Appendix

Appendix Contents

Introduction

What did investors who were Fools at heart do before there was a Motley Fool? Well, many of them participated — and still participate — in investment clubs.

Investing has long been something that people generally do not discuss amongst themselves. It was perceived as so mysterious and difficult that those without MBAs shouldn't try messing with it, lest they lose their entire nest egg in some silly blunder. Most people just closed their eyes and handed over their life savings to the Suspendered Ones on Wall Street, hoping for the best. Except for a small but growing band of merry investors, that is.

These exceptions to the rule were often members of investment clubs. They met regularly, discussing investing in general and various specific stocks. They pooled their money and plunged into the market. They took control of their own finances and did it… together. In many ways, investment clubs have been a precursor to Fooldom. Indeed, the Motley Fool has been called "the world's largest investment club."

At the core of Foolishness is community. Readers across the globe share thoughts, asking and answering questions in message boards, chats, and featured articles. Communities of Intel investors bat around opinions on the future of personal computing. People interested in Coca-Cola discuss how fast the company can grow and whether the stock is currently a good buy.

Most of this give and take occurs electronically in Fooldom, which is terrific. But there's also great value in investors meeting face-to-face to discuss companies and investing. And it's even better if these investors make a commitment to each other, to pool their time, money, and brainpower. The Motley Fool is now taking a huge step backward, toward the time-tested, rewarding tradition of investment clubs. Our online forum will continue to grow every day as we help you learn to make the most of your money. But we hereby invite you to supplement that learning by forming or joining an investment club.

Within these pages we offer you the nuts and bolts you'll need to begin your club experience — everything from picking a club name to selecting stocks to buy. Read through the information packed in here and consider whether starting or joining an investment club is something you might want to do.

Note: Please don't let the amount of information in here alarm, intimidate, or discourage you. Yes, there's some work and a lot of learning involved, but with investment clubs it's carried out in a fun group environment and you're never alone. Not all parts of this book will apply to you at this moment. You might want to focus on getting a club together before thinking about the steps involved in evaluating companies. Take what you need from this guide when you need it. Be assured that if you want to, you definitely *can* form a profitable and fun club and learn how to be a successful investor.

> Keep in mind as you read this primer that, to us, "Foolish" is a positive adjective. The Motley Fool gets its name from Shakespeare. In Elizabethan drama, the Fool is usually the only one who can tell the king the truth without losing his head — literally. We Fools aim to tell you the truth, too — that you can beat Wall Street at its own game. To learn more about the Motley Fool, drop by our website at www.fool.com or visit us on America Online at keyword: Fool.

Getting Started

Investment clubs have been around for decades and tens of thousands of them exist in America today. They've been growing in popularity in recent years, thanks to a lot of media coverage.

Members of investment clubs, often groups of friends or co-workers, typically meet once a month to discuss companies and make decisions about which stocks to buy and sell. At meetings they each contribute a small sum of money that is deposited in a club account. Members take turns researching and reporting on promising companies in which they might invest or companies in which the club is already invested.

The National Association of Investors Corp. (NAIC), established in 1951, has set forth guidelines for running successful investment clubs. It urges members to:

- Invest money regularly, regardless of market conditions
- Reinvest all dividends and capital gains
- Buy stock in companies that are growing faster than most of their peers
- Diversify investments, not putting all the communal eggs into one basket

Successful investment clubs focus on learning as well as doing. There's often an education officer elected and guest speakers are invited to the meetings. Club members seek to explore new ideas and discuss investing issues.

One month a member might present her findings on the value of screening for "low P/E" stocks. Another month, a member might report on a book he read about a great investor like Warren Buffett or Ben Graham. In the early sessions of a club's life, education components might be very introductory, covering how to read a company's balance sheet or earnings report. A year or two later, the club might be learning new ways to value stocks or discussing a published interview with a successful equities analyst.

Investment clubs today hold a total of more than $60 billion worth of equities in their portfolios — rivaling the largest mutual funds. Each month, investment clubs add about $50 million. This is big business — and exceedingly Foolish too, as it involves individual investors taking responsibility for their own investments.

Why Participate in an Investment Club?

Consider starting or joining an investment club if:

- You're new to investing and are looking for a good way to get your feet wet.
- You'd feel more comfortable learning about investing with others than on your own.
- You have roughly $20 to $50 that you can invest through the club each month.
- You've been putting off learning about investing and sense that having a responsibility to the group would provide some much-needed discipline.
- You think it would be fun to have a group of people with whom to share company research and to discuss investing topics.
- You're a woman and realize that you're likely to outlive your spouse and you have no idea how to handle the investments that he'll leave in your hands.
- Friends have gently suggested that it would be good for you to get out of the house once in a while.

⌒ Club Members Speak ⌒

When I first started our club, I knew absolutely nothing about stocks and my math skills were average to poor, but I did know that I wanted income in my retirement years. I am also a very social person, so when I first read of the Beardstown Ladies in a magazine, I knew that this was the direction in which I wanted to head.

Investment clubs serve as a terrific way for those new to investing to learn more about it in a friendly group setting. Many people are terrified of taking their first investing steps. Clubs make this relatively painless, as members cough up modest sums and invest carefully together after deliberating over the pros and cons of any action. After all, if two heads are better than one, imagine how much better a dozen or more heads can be. Making investment decisions is a lot less stressful when research work has been divided among members who have pooled not only their funds, but their experience and growing knowledge.

Many members eventually find that the clubs guide their own personal investing. After a while, their equity in the pooled club account may be relatively small compared with their separate personal accounts. Club meetings will offer many good ideas of attractive stocks in which to invest — and while the club may buy a few shares, members often go home and buy more shares for their own accounts. You may not have the time to research several stocks each month on your own, but by participating in a club, you'll share in the research of others and will have the extra bonus of a group setting in which to discuss investing ideas and issues.

Joining an Existing Club

Most investment clubs occasionally seek new members. Perhaps a member is moving away or is just unable to continue or — dare we say it? — perhaps a member has passed on to the great stock market in the sky. At times like these, new members may be invited to join.

You might expect that if a club's account has grown over a decade and its average member's equity is in the thousands of dollars that a new member would be expected to contribute a huge sum of money in order to join. Not true. The accounting systems that most clubs use permit new members to merely begin contributing the standard monthly amount. Longer-term members will each retain bigger pieces of the pie, and everyone's piece is calculated according to how much was contributed and when.

⌒ Club Members Speak ⌒

It's not always a good idea to join an existing club that's been around a long time, especially if you don't have a clue about investing. It can be very intimidating for the novice. Plus, if the group is very cohesive, you may feel like an outsider. And older clubs might not do the same in-depth research as new clubs do, with all the members anxious to learn.

Now that you might be all fired up at the prospect of joining an existing club, we'll hit you with some bad news. It can be hard to find the right club looking for a new member. Members of many of these clubs probably already have some friends they plan to invite. Your best bet might be to ask people you know whether they are in an investment club and if they need or anticipate needing any new bodies.

Alternatively, you can visit the Motley Fool's online message folders. Go to our "Folly in 50 States" area and post a message in your state's folder saying that you're looking to join a club.

Once you find a club to join, take the time to learn more about it before signing up. Consider questions such as the following:

- Do you get along with the other members? (If many of them seem too quiet, obnoxious, young, aggressive, meek, tall, wishy-washy, or Wise, this might not be the best group for you.)

- Do you have goals in common? (Perhaps you are risk-averse and want to invest in more stable blue-chip stocks, but they're aggressively out to find volatile, quickly growing small companies.)

- Is the regular contribution too steep for you? ($60 per month, for example, means $720 per year. This can be a lot for some people.)

- Do you have the same basic investing philosophy? (If you're a true Fool, you probably won't want to belong to a club that relies mainly on technical analysis, just looks for stocks that are going to split, or doesn't do its own research, preferring to rely on the recommendations of gurus. Yuck!)

> ### ⌒ Club Members Speak ⌒
>
> *The success of any club depends on what each individual member brings to it. Be particular about who comes into the club. We don't recruit members; we let them come to us. We know that they are very interested.*

How to Start a Club

If you can't find a suitable club, or even if you'd rather not look, you still have a viable alternative: Start your own investment club.

There are many steps involved in getting an investment club up and running, but fret not — most of them are relatively straightforward. Following is a list to guide you as you assemble a club.

Start talking with friends and see who's interested. It's best to gather a variety of people who will bring to the club a variety of interests, experiences, and perspectives. Once you find a few interested friends, let them invite a few of their own friends. Aim to form a club with roughly 12 to 15 members, give or take a few. Anything from 10 to 20 should work well, and a few more or less can also work. Too few and you may have trouble accumulating funds to invest. Too many and you'll have trouble having quality discussions and finding a place to meet.

Distribute information about investment clubs to anyone who has expressed interest. (Hey! You could even buy more copies of this

primer and pass them out to interested folks.) You want people to learn
what investment clubs are all about and think about whether they're really
interested.

Gather all interested parties for a preliminary meeting. Meet to
discuss (A) whether you have enough in common, (B) how you'll be
organized and run, and (C) whether people are still seriously interested
in forming a club. The following items are things that you should try to
agree on. It might be good to go around the room and get everyone's
thoughts on each of these issues.

Make sure that everyone joining is committed to the enterprise.
You can formalize the commitment by including a clause in your partnership agreement that requires each member to agree to stick it out for at
least a year. Some clubs even require deposits, but this isn't always necessary.

Make sure that you all have similar or compatible investing goals. If
some people want to double their money in two years and then get out,
that's not only unrealistic, but also probably at odds with those who want to
learn and slowly grow their savings.

Agree on the amount of the monthly minimum contribution. You
don't have to set this as high as possible. Remember that this is a learning
activity, and you can always increase the amount at a later date. Many
clubs allow members to contribute more than the monthly minimum level
if they so desire. Also, contributions to the club shouldn't necessarily be
the only investment you make. You might be contributing $25 per month to
your investment club, but putting aside $150 per month for your personal
savings and investing. (Indeed, you can even set up your club so that no
money is ever collected, except for pizza — see the section on "Faux
Investment Clubs.")

**To the degree that you can, agree on some common ground
regarding a general investing philosophy and approach.** As an example, perhaps you agree that Warren Buffett's approach is one you'd like to

incorporate or emulate. Maybe many of you believe in Foolish investing tenets. Perhaps some want to find significantly undervalued stocks, while others want to find high-flying stocks. Differences don't necessarily represent a death knell, but it's good to start out knowing how everyone feels. And besides, many investment styles are not diametrically opposed. Fools and Warren Buffett have much common ground. It's also a good idea not to restrict yourselves too much. Only investing in ultraconservative stocks might be boring. You can add some excitement by plunking a few dollars into some more dynamic companies — in the best-case scenario you'll profit, and in the worst-case you'll learn a few extra lessons. Ultimately, your main common ground should be a desire to learn and to make money.

Agree on a set of common-ground references, instructions, tools, and/or readings. Dare we be presumptuous enough to suggest that *The Motley Fool Investment Guide* or the "13 Steps to Investing Foolishly" could be such references? (Yes, we dare!) Peter Lynch's *One Up on Wall Street, Beating the Street*, and *Learn to Earn* are some other fine and easily understandable works. (FoolMart has assembled a large group of books that pass Foolish muster, organized by difficulty and also listed A-Z. You'll find them online at www.foolmart.com.) You might even all agree to subscribe to a certain magazine, such as *SmartMoney*; a certain newspaper, such as *Investor's Business Daily*; or to regularly read the Motley Fool's Evening News and Fool Portfolio reports. This way, you'll all have some reading in common and you can discuss articles or issues of interest.

Make sure that every member understands that it's possible to lose money when investing. Even the best investors make mistakes. Members should be prepared to start out losing money — something that's likely should the market take a temporary tumble. Just remember that in the long run, the best place to park your moolah is in stocks.

Agree on a regular meeting time, place, length, and format. One reason to try to keep a club size to around 10 to 15 people is that it allows you to hold meetings in living rooms. Another possibility is to seek out some other space, like a local library, church, coffeehouse, or watering hole. Perhaps a member has an available meeting room at his workplace. Decide when you'll meet, and how often. Most clubs meet once a month. For the format, outline the various items of business you plan to cover at each meeting and allocate a certain amount of time for each. This will help you keep meetings running efficiently and prevent someone's report from going on for an hour and dragging things out too long. Most meetings will probably last between one and three hours.

Agree on snacks. Snacks can be a very important part of any meeting. In unfortunate situations, they might even be what meeting attendees look forward to most. Your club can choose to bypass snacks — or you can decide to take turns bringing donuts or fancy cheeses.

You'll need a name for the club. You can be straightforward and name the club after something like your geographical region, or you can be creative. Names that some clubs have used include: The Money Makers, The Small Wonder Investment Group, Blue Chips and Salsa, The Common Bond Investment Club, Common Cents, The Fortune Seekers, The Steady Plodders, The Live and Learn Investors, The Silk STOCKings Investment Club, Stocks and Bonding, Blooming Assets, Lady Investigators, The Hounds of Xemba, The Stockettes, Fortune Hunters, Dynavestors, and so on.

One group of women named their club the Stroke of Luck because they all met at a doctor's office after their husbands had strokes, leaving the women suddenly needing to take control of the family finances.

We've covered a lot of ground so far. If this has taken a long while, you could close the first meeting and resume organizational discussions at the next. There's no rush. Below are more (yes, more) things to settle as you set up your club.

Agree on how you'll be organized legally and operationally. The simplest thing to do might seem to be nothing, keeping your club's accounts under one member's name and social security number. This can turn into a tax and accounting nightmare, though, as you try to transfer gains and losses to members. This is why most investment clubs choose to be partnerships, with accounts registered under the club's unique tax identification number. (In the Appendix, we have included sample club bylaws and a partnership agreement.) Don't neglect this paperwork — it's vital. For your club to be recognized as a legal entity, there are forms to fill out. In addition, realize that your $20 or $50 initial contributions will be growing into a significant pile of wealth. You'll want to have formal agreements in place to protect yourselves in case one member turns out to be a dastardly demon.

Get a Tax Identification Number for your club. One of you should contact either the IRS (800-829-1040) or your local U.S. Treasury office and request Form SS-4. (A sample of the form is included in the

Appendix.) Fill it out, including the name of your club and the names, addresses, and social security numbers of club officers. This number is important. You'll be including it on any tax filings, and it will be required for your club's brokerage account. Club members will need to include the number when reporting club income on their individual tax returns.

As part of the previous discussion, you'll have determined how your club will be organized — or at least will have begun talking about it. Finish that conversation now. Agree on what responsibilities there are, and what officers you'll need to elect to take on these responsibilities. Clarify what the responsibilities of the officers, as well as club members, will be. (Remember that even regular, non-officer members have responsibilities.) Elect your officers in one of the first meetings. Typical clubs have:

- A president/presiding partner, who sets meetings, presides over them, and plans activities.

- A vice president/assistant presiding partner, who fills in when needed and might also run the education program.

- A financial partner/treasurer, who deals with the brokerage, buys and sells stock, and keeps records of the club's holdings as well as each member's share. (This needs to be a careful, detail-oriented, and responsible person. In fact, since this is the most difficult job, it might even be shared by two people.)

- A recording partner/secretary, who keeps minutes of each meeting, reminds members of meetings when necessary, and possibly mails out minutes to members who miss a meeting.

- Some clubs have a separate education officer, responsible for planning (with the input of the group) an educational program, which might include presentations, field trips, guest speakers, and assigned reading.

Since you're likely to be a Foolish club, though, you might come up with some more inspired names for officers. For example:

- Big Kahuna
- Not-Quite-as-Big Kahuna
- High Priestess of Learning
- Foofah of Finances
- Head Honcho of Minutes and Agendas
- Superintendent of Snacks

Assign someone to look into choosing a broker. The NAIC seems to favor full-service brokers, encouraging clubs to find a broker they like and can work with who'll provide some advice and guidance and perhaps even attend meetings on occasion. Contrary to this, Fools opt for discount brokers. We'd like to see you learning enough to make your own investment decisions. If you're calling your own shots, you don't need to pay hefty commissions to full-service brokerages. Discuss the differences between full-service and discount brokers and decide which you prefer. Consider taking advantage of the incredibly low commissions offered for online trading by discount brokers. Several are in the neighborhood of $8 per trade. At our website, we have a "Discount Brokerage Center"— see "Resources" in the Appendix.

Decide on an educational agenda. This will naturally change a bit over time as you become more sophisticated investors. But it's important to start out with some kind of plan. Perhaps you want to take the first few months to learn how to read annual reports. If you're already comfortable with that, you might delve into various valuation methods. Discuss topics of interest and set up a plan for learning. A good way to start this discussion might be to go around the room and ask members to say what big questions they have about investing that they'd like answers to. If members think this would be too embarrassing, you could all write down lists of these questions anonymously and then collect and discuss them. (No one should be embarrassed, though — your club should foster an open and non-intimidating atmosphere.)

Make a list of member interests and expertise. Here's why. As you begin hunting for companies in which to invest, you'll want to choose industries to study. As both Peter Lynch and the Brothers Gardner like to point out, it's a great strategy to "buy what you know." (Actually, it's probably best restated as "research what you know.") If you're in the chemical business, you might volunteer to look into companies in that industry, choosing a few for a close look. If a member is an avid golfer, she might look into golf-related companies. It's a good idea to make a list of the industries with which your club members are familiar. Even if someone's only hobby is hitting the malls every weekend, that's a great boon — he'll be familiar with many retailers.

Finally, agree to have fun and to keep your meetings friendly and cooperative. And please consider dropping us a note now and then with any experiences, suggestions, or even funny stories you'd care to share. Perhaps your group came up with some clever officer titles? Let's hear 'em! Via email, you can reach us at: InvClub@fool.com.

Running Your Investment Club

Forming an investment club can seem like the hardest part of the entire club process. While this may indeed be true, don't let yourself give short shrift to running your club. Remember that club meetings are just that — meetings. And while it may be hard for five percent of the population to believe, ninety-five percent of Americans don't love meetings.

The ideal investment club meeting should be managed efficiently, should be friendly and fun, and should leave some time for socializing. In the next section we'll cover some tips for running meetings smoothly.

General Meeting Tips

Be punctual. Realize that there are early birds and latecomers in almost every group. If you hold up the meeting waiting for the latecomers, you'll annoy the early birds and will eventually end up with the latecomers arriving even later. If you're scheduled to start the meeting at 7 p.m., start at 7 p.m. Latecomers will learn that if they don't want to miss out on any business, they'll need to be on time.

Be organized. This will help the meeting move along smoothly. Pass out copies of the agenda. Have someone distribute minutes of the last meeting. If this seems like too much, the minuteman (hey — there's a great title) could at least quickly summarize the last meeting orally. It always helps to know where you're going and where you've been. In addition, if members see that there are nine items on the agenda, they might be less inclined to go off on a long tangent on item number two.

Be swift. Consider having a member act as timekeeper. If time limits are assigned to each agenda item, then the timekeeper can make sure the group remains on track, perhaps issuing two-minute warnings when it's almost time to move on to the next item.

Be orderly. Find a system of order that works well with your group. Traditionalists might opt for the time-tested Robert's Rules of Order (summarized in inexpensive books you can get through your favorite bookseller), while more avant-garde groups might invent their own systems. Just make sure that everyone has a chance to be heard on every topic and that no one dominates discussions and decisions.

Be fun. If your club is running at 99% efficiency, it might be stifling a few jokes that some members would like to inject. Sacrifice just a little efficiency, if need be, to maintain a sense of fun — and Folly.

The Agenda

Here is a sample agenda for a meeting. Look it over and then we'll review some of its key components. Keep in mind that your club's agenda may differ. (You'll find a sample of an actual club agenda along with interesting ways the club has promoted its club meetings in the Appendix.)

- Distribute agenda for present meeting and minutes of last meeting
- Bring out snacks
- Review treasurer report on current club finances
- Present educational component
- Collect monthly contributions
- Discuss/review any important issues about current holdings
- Discuss stock ideas to study for possible purchase
- Choose one industry to focus on for the next meeting
- Assign stocks to study for the next meeting to various members
- Present and discuss stocks assigned at the last meeting
- Discuss what transactions to make this month
- Raise and discuss any new business or follow up on any old issues
- Plan topics for the next meeting

The Treasurer Report

Your treasurer should be prepared at each meeting to review the club's current financial situation. (In the event that the treasurer can't make a meeting, the information should be passed on to another club member to present.) The club members should be updated on:

- The current value of the portfolio — in total and broken out by holdings
- The current value of each member's "account," or share of the pie
- Any major changes in any values since the last meeting (such as stock splits, dividends, and spin-offs)
- Transactions executed since the last meeting

The Educational Component

This component will vary widely according to the level of investing experience of the members as well as member interests. Here are some suggested educational activities:

A member could present a summary of a book he or she has read. This might be a biography of a great investor, a book on business strategy by a successful CEO, a close look at a particular industry, or a book detailing some aspect of investing. Visit FoolMart online at www.foolmart.com for ideas of books that we like and recommend.

Examples of books you can learn a lot from include: *Buffett: The Making of an American Capitalist* (Roger Lowenstein), *Built to Last: Successful Habits of Visionary Companies* (James C. Collins & Jerry I. Porras), *Beating the Street* (Peter Lynch), and *The Motley Fool Investment Guide* (David & Tom Gardner). If many of your members are new to reading annual reports, you each might get a copy of *How to Read a Financial Report* (by John A. Tracy). Then you can read and discuss a chapter or two at a time, helping each other digest and understand the information.

- A member, having read up on some aspect of valuing companies, might teach the group how to calculate and interpret a certain financial ratio, such as the Price-to-Sales Ratio. Some worksheets could be handed out and everyone can practice crunching the numbers.

- Everyone could have agreed the week before to read a certain article or a chapter in a particular book. Take the time now in the meeting to discuss it. It might be a magazine article focusing on fees charged by mutual funds or one on the growth of the personal computer industry. You might even discuss articles of interest from the Motley Fool website.

- You might go through the financial statements in a company's annual report together, discussing which numbers are significant and calculating some ratios.

Remember — as long as all your members are not comfortable with such financial reports, your club will never reach its potential. It's absolutely fine if you all start out knowing nothing about investing, but you need to get to the point where you're all able to read financial statements and make some sense of them without breaking into a cold sweat. The Fool is here to help you master such things.

Collect Monthly Contributions

This is the point when everyone chips in the agreed-upon amount of cash for the club coffers. Depending on your initial agreement, some members might contribute a little more than the usual sum. If any members are unable to attend, they should still send in their contribution, perhaps with someone else. For those who are not ready with the money, some clubs charge a late fee. This could be deposited into a "fun" account for buying tasty treats, or it could go toward general club operational expenses, such as paying an accountant to prepare tax forms.

Discuss Current Holdings

Take a few minutes to discuss any developments regarding the stocks currently in your portfolio. It's a good idea to assign each stock to a club member, so that the member is responsible for following the company and reporting on any important developments. Since you each own a small part of these companies, you need to understand what's going on with them.

You'll also want to regularly review each holding to make sure that you still want to hold it. If the reasons you bought it are no longer valid, you might do well to sell. Or the stock price might have risen so much lately that it has become overvalued. (Note that some clubs will want to stick with a very long-term buy-and-hold strategy, while others might elect to trade more often.) Whatever valuation and analysis methods you apply to a stock you're considering buying should also be applied to stocks you own, and you should assess these stocks periodically.

Discuss Stocks for Possible Purchase

At some point in your meeting, you should discuss any stock ideas members have. These might include a company whose products club members buy regularly, an interesting company written about in a magazine or newspaper, a "hot tip" deemed worthy of further investigation, or a company discovered through some stock screening system.

You can also get some good ideas from the Fool website. We write about interesting companies every day and have literally thousands of message folders where Fools discuss individual companies.

Once you've batted around some ideas, you might approach stock picking by looking at the *industry* of your next purchase. Let's say you discussed an automaker, a clothing retailer, and a biotech firm. If the most promising or intriguing company is the clothing retailer, then look at that industry next. Remember that you don't want to examine a company in a vacuum, without comparing it to its peers. If the initial company was Gap, Inc., choose a few of its peers to study also. These might include The Limited, Lands' End, Guess? Inc., Donna Karan, and The TJX Cos.

Once you have the industry and the peer group of three to six companies, assign each company to a club member. In the early months of your club's existence, if all members are not comfortable studying stocks on their own, you might assign each company to pairs or small groups of members. You could choose a group of three companies and have groups of three or four people study each one.

Whoever is assigned to study one of the companies should plan to report back to the group at the next monthly meeting, offering an analysis of the company and a recommendation as to whether it would be a good stock to buy. Don't think that, in the example above, only Gap, Inc. should be evaluated as a possible purchase. Evaluate all the companies in the group. After all, your interest might have initially been drawn to Gap, but after studying a bunch of similar companies, you might discover that Lands' End is a much more promising stock.

A Foolish product that might be of use to you is our *Industry Snapshot*, which introduces readers to a different industry every two weeks, discussing key players in the sector and highlighting the company that seems most interesting in the group.

Discuss Stocks Assigned for Study

Once the next meeting rolls around, members who were assigned a company to study will make their presentations. It's important that everyone in the group be able to look at the data as it's discussed, so handouts should be prepared and passed out. These might include:

- Recent company financial reports to look over. (We explain how to get these later.)
- A summary of the company, its history, and current operations. (You can get some terrific company reports at www.hoovers.com if you subscribe to their service.)

- Results of the club member's number crunching, featuring various ratios and valuation estimates. (Again, more information on this to follow.)

This part of your meeting should be part show-and-tell and part discussion of analysis. For the show-and-tell element, the presenter might pass around samples of the company's main products, if possible. If this isn't possible, he or she could show samples of the company's advertisements, which reveal how the company is describing itself and its products.

In addition to discussing the numbers, you want to make sure to discuss the competitive environment for the industry. Figure out which companies compete directly with each other. Who's gaining market share and who's losing it? How is the media covering the industry — is one company consistently portrayed as the leader?

Once each company in the group has been presented, take a little time to look at them all together and compare them. See which one, *if any*, appears to be the best candidate for investment. Realize that you don't necessarily have to invest in any of them. Perhaps all of them seem overvalued right now. You might decide to add one or two to a "watch list" and keep an eye on them, in case they drop in price in the future.

Decide on Transactions

Once you've reviewed and discussed the month's crop of stocks, you'll need to decide where to put the month's money. You have several choices. You can:

- Invest it in the most promising company reviewed at this meeting.
- Invest it in one or more of your current holdings. If none of the companies discussed this month are as attractive as one you invested in last month, you might just want to plunk more money into that company this time (assuming that it remains attractive).
- Invest in a recently studied company that has been on your group's watch list and has fallen in price to an attractive level.
- Invest in a combination of the above options.
- Do nothing. Leave the money in your brokerage account until you find the right place to invest it.

Close the Meeting

Before disbanding, there are a few things your group should do:

- Raise and discuss any new items of business
- Follow up on any old issues from prior meetings

- Plan topics for the next meeting(s), including any educational components
- See if members have concerns to raise or questions to ask
- Confirm where and when the next meeting will be held
- Verify who's bringing snacks to the next meeting

> ### ☜ Club Members Speak ☞
>
> *In a typical meeting, our club will address "Old Business," which includes stocks we have talked about in the past, and "New Business" — new stocks and other business. We'll also play a game — perhaps a trivia challenge or something related to the people in the room, our stocks, or just thought questions. I try and use esteem building techniques (we all need that). For instance, next month I will ask everyone to write down one characteristic that they admire about the person sitting on their left and one characteristic that they wish they could change about themselves. It is very thought provoking and it brings our group closer together. It is always near the end of the meeting, so we leave with a smile.*

Member Turnover

An issue that will have to be addressed now and then is member turnover. You will invariably lose a member on occasion to the grim reaper (sad but true), ennui (heaven forfend!), or perhaps the FBI witness protection program (stranger things have happened… we think).

When this happens, the departing member (or beneficiary) will be due his or her share of the club account. How it's distributed to the member should depend on the agreement you all signed. There's usually the option of paying the member in cash and/or stock. If cash is chosen, you'll all have to decide how many shares of which stocks to sell to generate the correct amount of cash. Note that any capital gains realized by the sale should be spread out among all members according to their share of ownership.

It's often preferable to pay the departing member in stock instead of cash. This is because, rather than being sold and generating taxes, the stocks are merely transferred. The club does not pay any taxes and the departing member doesn't either, until the shares are sold. (Prior to transferring shares, if the member doesn't have an account with the club brokerage, it might be worth opening one — that way the shares will be transferred most expeditiously.)

Sometimes a member might need to withdraw part of his or her share. For such a partial withdrawal, you'll go through the same procedure as above.

When your club loses a member, you'll have to decide whether you want to take on a new one. As years go by, you'll probably find that many friends and acquaintances will express interest in joining your club. It might be a good idea to keep a list of these people.

For more information on new members joining existing clubs, see the section in this primer called "Joining an Existing Club."

Keeping Interest High

We've got some good news and bad news for you. First, the bad: If you don't keep interest high, your club won't survive. Even worse, it'll die a slow, agonizing death, bereft of dignity, gasping for air, and making strange, unpleasant noises.

Yikes. Let's move on quickly to the good news: It's not that hard to keep interest high. In fact, a little attention to this part of your club's life will make the whole experience even more fun. Here are some ideas and suggestions.

Take field trips. There's no rule that an investment club's life should only exist within the confines of a living room. There's much exploration and learning to be had beyond your usual walls.

If you're near a stock exchange, visit it. In Manhattan, for example, the New York Stock Exchange (NYSE) allows visitors to view the trading floor and features an "Interactive Education Center." Reservations are required for groups larger than ten, and more information can be found at the NYSE website at www.nyse.com. Fools living near San Francisco can visit the Pacific Stock Exchange there. Other sites, like the Philadelphia Stock Exchange and the Chicago Stock Exchange, also offer tours. Just give them a call.

You can also visit other financial services businesses, such as brokerages or banks. Call one close to you, explain that your investment club would like to learn more about what goes on there, and see if a tour can be arranged.

It might seem surprising, but your group could get a lot out of a field trip to your local library. Call and arrange it ahead of time and ask the reference librarian to show you all the resources you can tap when researching companies. If you have access to a large library in your region — perhaps even a university or business school library — you'll find even more information available to you. Remember that it's a reference librarian's job to help you conduct your research. Give them a chance to do what they were trained to do.

If any companies you've invested in have headquarters close to you, consider attending the annual shareholder meeting. This is a great opportunity to meet the folks running the company and get a feel for where the company is headed. Even at another time of the year, the company might be able to arrange for you to meet with some employees (perhaps someone in investor relations) and tour the offices or — better yet — a factory or plant.

Similarly, if you're considering investing in a local company, call the investor relations department and try to arrange a meeting. If you're considering investing in a national retail chain, you can probably find a store to visit within driving distance. For example, if Home Depot looks good to you on paper, head over to one of its outlets and see how the store operates. You can even do some market research. Count how many customers enter the doors and then compare this with a competitor. Ask some customers why they shop there and if they're likely to return. Watch to see how much people are spending in the store. (You can have a lot of fun on such a reconnaissance mission — wear trench coats and fedoras, take copious notes, and glance at each other furtively. See if you're asked to leave.)

Stage a debate. If club member Thelma often brings up the idea of investing in Three Initial Corp., but fellow club member Charlie always shoots it down quickly, let them prepare and deliver cases for and against such a purchase. They can each offer a rebuttal to the other's arguments and then everyone can vote on who was more persuasive. Perhaps you'll end up deciding to further research and eventually buy shares of Three Initial Corp.

Communicate with other clubs. You can do this electronically by posting and reading messages in our message folders dedicated to investment clubs. (See "Resources" in the Appendix.) You can also do it in person. Find some clubs located near you and have a few members of your club visit their club meetings and invite them to visit yours. You can locate local clubs through our "Folly in 50 States" message boards as well as the message boards we maintain for individual investment clubs. This is a great way to share good ideas and lessons on what works and what doesn't work.

Socialize. Your entire club, perhaps including spouses, could go out for a nice dinner. Or maybe one member can have everyone over to his house to watch a movie. *Wall Street* comes to mind as an example, as does *Barbarians at the Gate*. *The Hudsucker Proxy* and *Trading Places* can also be fun. A wonderful classic is Judy Holliday's 1956 film *The Solid Gold Cadillac*, in which she champions the rights of the small investor. (Of course, since this is meant to be a purely social evening, you can pick a movie totally unrelated to money and investing.) Your group can even host another investment club for a joint cocktail party.

Seek out interesting issues to explore. Encourage club members to clip out and copy articles for each other. This will enhance the ongoing education of all members as well as provide for some interesting discussions.

Games are another great way to keep a good measure of fun in your club. You might hold a mock portfolio contest, with members picking the ten stocks they think will do best in the next few months or year. One member can be in charge of reporting each month on who's winning the contest. Members can also compete against each other at websites like the Hollywood Stock Exchange (www.hsx.com), where you buy and sell movie stocks and movie star bonds.

⌒ Club Members Speak ⌒

I don't like a club with a format that is too formal. Most clubs break up within three years. This is, in part, due to the fact that most members work and have families to care for and don't feel they can put in hours of research time. By being less formal, the members in the clubs I have started to look forward to meetings, don't feel pressured if they didn't have time to do research and are more willing to get involved and contribute ideas. As for snacks, have potluck dinners and serve wine. Sometimes we just do desserts and coffee. Twice a year we have a BBQ with spouses. Have a great name, too — it's half the fun.

Guest speakers can also invigorate a club. You can invite employees of interesting companies, experienced investors, bankers, economists, college professors, or anyone who can discuss trends in a particular industry. Perhaps a friend of yours works for a major bookstore chain. He could come to your club and discuss his impressions of where the publishing industry is headed. If an acquaintance works for a high-tech firm, she could come and perhaps explain a little bit about the semiconductor equipment or networking industry to your group. Enter our occasional Fool contests, and your club might even win a chance to have Motley Fool co-founder David or Tom Gardner address your club.

Take your club online. Read more about this in a following section.

Tracking Your Results and Keeping Records

Tracking your results and keeping accurate records can be the most difficult part of running an investment club. Indeed, this is where the famous Beardstown Ladies fell short. It can be easy to make a mistake here or there, and that's what happened to them. But it doesn't have to happen to you.

As an individual investor, tracking your performance is relatively simple. If you have $5,000 in your account at the beginning of the year and end the year with $6,000, a little basic math will show you how much your investment grew:

Calculating Investment Growth

$6000 (ending value) minus $5000 (starting value) equals $1000 (total gain for the period)

$1000 divided by $5000 (starting value) equals 0.20

To convert 0.20 to a percentage, multiply by 100, which gives us 20% — and that's how much your investment grew.

Unfortunately, things get more complicated if you're continually adding money to your portfolio. And that's what investment clubs (and many individual investors) do — add money each month. On top of this, clubs have many people and everyone doesn't always add the same amount each month. And over the years people leave and join the club, so each member's piece of the pie doesn't always end up being the same size.

What's a club to do? Well, one good option is to use accounting software developed specifically for investment club accounting. NAIC offers club accounting software, and the Motley Fool plans to release its own investment club accounting software, ClubTrak, in the summer of 1998.

One way of solving this problem is for each member to have an equal share in the club. This means that everyone has to contribute the same amount of money at each meeting. The advantage here is that accounting stays relatively simple. For example, if the club has 12 members, to calculate any member's equity, you just divide the club's worth by 12. Simple. The main disadvantage, though, occurs when a new member joins (perhaps replacing a departing member). If each member's share is $5,000 at that time, the new member will have to cough up that amount in order to remain on equal ground with the others.

The club accounting method recommended by the NAIC is the "unit value system." It's very much like the system used by mutual funds, which have to adjust every day for deposits and withdrawals. The system takes the total club portfolio and divides it into equally priced shares, or "units." Each member is credited with an appropriate number of units. As time goes on, money is continually deposited into the account and the portfolio's value grows due to those contributions and the appreciation (we hope!) of the stocks in the portfolio. Each month, the unit price is readjusted.

Here's a rough example of how it works:

— Fifteen members each contribute $25 in the first month. The club fund holds $375. This is divided into 15 unit shares, valued at $25 each. Each member at this point is credited with one share.

— The club buys 20 shares of stock in company ABC. Shares are priced at $17.50 each — for a total of $350. This leaves a $10 in cash in the account (after a $15 brokerage commission).

— A month later, the financial officer prepares the monthly report for the club. At this time, the 20 shares of stock are worth $19 each, or a total of $380. Plus, there's the $10 cash, so the entire club account is worth $390.

— When $390 is divided by the 15 existing unit shares, we learn that each share is now worth $26.

— At the next meeting, members again contribute money. Let's say that 13 of them contribute the usual $25, but two of them contribute $40. (A total of $405.)

— These contributions will buy each member additional unit shares in the club — but remember — each share is now worth $26. So a contribution of $25 will buy 0.96 of a share. (Don't freak out if these numbers seem scary to you. This is still simple math here. 25 divided by 26 equals 0.96.) Each $40 contribution will buy 1.54 shares. (40 divided by 26 = 1.54)

— So 13 people get 0.96 shares each, for a total of 12.48 shares. (13 times 0.96 equals 12.48.) Add to this the two people who each get 1.54 shares and you have a total of 15.56 new shares.

So the club now has:

Stock ABC
　　20 shares, valued last at $19 ea. total:　　　$380
Cash remaining prior to this meeting:　　　　　　$ 10
Cash deposited at this meeting:　　　　　　　　　$405
Current total:　　　　　　　　　　　　　　　　　$795

That is the club account's value in stock and cash. Below is its value in unit shares:

	Number of shares	Value each	Total value
Initial unit shares:	15.00	$25	$375
Added at next meeting	15.56	$26	$405
Current total:	30.56 x	$26 =	$795

Notice that the $795 is not the total of $375 and $405. Instead, it's the total number of shares multiplied by their latest value.

Let's go through one more month to see what happens next.

— At this same meeting, let's say that the members agree to buy stock XYZ. They can afford to buy 18 shares, which are currently trading at $22 each. The financial officer places the order the next day. 18 times 22 equals 396. So that means $396 is subtracted from the club's cash hoard of $415, leaving $19.

— A month later, just before the next meeting, the financial officer is preparing her report for the members. Company ABC reported weaker-than-expected earnings and shares dropped to $16 each. But company XYZ, purchased at $22 per share, is now trading at $23 per share.

So now, the group has the following assets:

Stock ABC
　　20 shares, valued last at $16 ea. total:　　　$320
Stock XYZ
　　18 shares, valued last at $23 ea. total:　　　$414
Cash remaining prior to this meeting:　　　　　　$ 19
Current value of club account:　　　　　　　　　$753

The club has 30.56 unit shares. If you divide $753 by 30.56, you arrive at the new value of each unit share: $24.64. This means that at the upcoming meeting, each $25 deposit will buy 1.015 shares (25 divided by 24.64 equals 1.015.)

— At the meeting, each member contributes $25, gaining 1.015 shares. So the total deposit is $375 (15 x 25 = 375), and 15.225 shares (15 x 1.015 = 15.225).

Here's the new club accounting at the end of the meeting (before any new shares of stock are purchased with the cash balance):

Stock ABC
    20 shares, valued @ $16 ea. total: $320
Stock XYZ
    18 shares, valued @ $23 ea. total: $414
Cash remaining prior to this meeting: $ 19
Cash deposited at this meeting: $375
Current value of club account $1,128

	Number of shares	Value each	Total value
Initial unit shares:	15.00	$25	$375
Added at next mtg:	15.56	$26	$405
And at the meeting after:	15.225	$24.64	$375
Current total:	45.785 x	$24.64 =	$1,128

By now, you should have a sense of how it works. This method might seem complicated, but it really isn't, once you get used to it. And it has a bunch of advantages. It makes it easy for any member to know how much his personal share of the account is worth.

For example, someone who contributed $25 at each of the three meetings would have bought 1 unit share, then 0.96 of a unit share, and then 1.015 of a unit share. He would have a total of 2.975 unit shares which, at the current value of $24.64, are worth $73.30.

By dividing $73.30 by the club's total value of $1,128, he would see that he owns 6.5% of the club. (He could reach the same conclusion by dividing his 2.975 shares by the club's total of 45.785 shares.)

Remember that the two members who contributed more than $25 one week will each have a slightly greater piece of the pie. They'll have 3.555 shares each, worth $87.60.

Using this system, it's easy if someone wants to leave or join your club. A new member simply contributes the $25 (or whatever) and gets however many shares (or whatever fraction of a share) that amount will buy. At that point, veteran members might each have dozens of unit shares, but the new member will have only a few. This is fair, considering that the veteran members have been contributing for a long time. The system also makes it easy if a member can't contribute one week — he or she just doesn't contribute and isn't credited with any additional shares. That's it.

The system also makes it easy to calculate your club's performance. Just measure the changing value of the unit shares. If the unit shares were originally valued at $25 each and a year later they were worth $28, you can use the math introduced at the beginning of this section to see what kind of return this represents:

Calculating Returns Using Unit Shares

$28 (ending value) minus $25 (starting value) equals $3 (gain for the period)

$3 divided by $25 (starting value) equals 0.12

To convert 0.12 to a percentage, multiply by 100, which gives us 12% — and that's how much your investment grew.

If this section is still making your head spin, consider approaching a member of a more experienced club to see if anyone in that club is willing to help your club get up to speed with accounting. (It seems that some experienced club members actually manage the accounting of newer clubs — for a fee.) You can also go to the Fool's Investment Club message folder and get advice from club members there.

The most important thing might be to make sure that your group has chosen a math-friendly person to be your financial record-keeper. You want the person to be comfortable with basic math (and good at it, too!).

Clubs and Taxes

Taxes can be confusing enough for individuals filling out 1040 forms. They get a little more complicated for investment clubs. (But not *too* complicated — keep reading!)

First of all, your club will probably be organized as a partnership and, as mentioned earlier, will have applied for and received a "tax identification number." Partnerships, according to the NAIC, are the simplest option for tax reporting.

In a partnership, the partnership itself doesn't pay any taxes. Instead, each member pays taxes individually. The partnership's income is reported to the IRS by the club treasurer, who files Form 1065 in April.

Attached to it is a Schedule K-1 for each member, detailing the member's allocation of income and expenses according to the partnership arrangement. In other words, if the partnership agreement is that each member will have an equal share, then club income and expenses will be divided equally among members. If the partnership has allowed some members to contribute more and take bigger stakes, then the K-1 should reflect their share accurately.

Each club member gets a copy of the K-1 to file with his or her own personal tax return. This, along with Schedule D, will show the member's gains or losses. We've included samples of Form 1065 and Schedule K-1 in the Appendix of this primer.

Your club might want to have an accountant or other tax professional prepare (or at least review) your paperwork. This is fine, but realize that just as with personal tax forms, the filer (and not the professional) is still responsible for the content of the return. Regardless of who prepares the paperwork, it's probably smart to have someone double-check the information. Or better yet, perhaps a second person can prepare the forms independently. They can then be compared.

To fill out these forms, you'll need records of exactly when each stock was purchased and/or sold, the price at which the transaction occurred, and the holding's current value.

Although the tax form preparation might seem daunting, you don't have to do it alone. You can tap the experience of older clubs or post questions online in the Fool's Investment Club message folder. Also helpful is the NAIC's club accounting software. (We'll soon be releasing ClubTrak, the Foolish investment club accounting software.)

Kinds of Clubs

Make Your Club Foolish

You won't find many Fools disagreeing with most National Association of Investors Corp. (NAIC) guidelines. They're quite sensible. But we hereby propose that you take traditional NAIC-style investment clubs a step further… and make them Foolish.

Foolish clubs are encouraged to take advantage of cyberspace, where the resources of message boards and instant data retrieval make research and communication easier. As your club strives to learn more about investing, we hope that you'll find Foolish materials (most available free online) helpful.

One challenge investment clubs face is keeping everyone interested and motivated. The amusing and informative articles in Fooldom can be very effective when shared and discussed in a group setting.

If your club members have all read at least one of the Fool books or our "13 Steps to Investing Foolishly," you will have a grounding in our Foolosophy to help you separate the good from the bad out there. There are many books, pundits, and seminars eager to grab your attention and your wallet as they promise you great rewards. Know where to draw the line. Don't fall prey to technical analysis mumbo jumbo or active-trading, get-rich-quick schemes.

Remember that you should try to consider a company in the context of its industry. Compare it to its peers. Evaluate it as an ongoing business, not just a chart of historical performance. Find and buy great companies and hold them for the long term. Don't sacrifice gains to the churning and commission gods. Compare your performance to a benchmark like the Standard & Poor's 500 Stock Index. If you stick to investing fundamentals and actively participate in our online forum, you should do well.

Take Your Club Online

When we urge you to take your club online, we don't mean that you should necessarily go to the extreme of having a solely online club, where you never meet face-to-face. There's great value in face-to-face club meetings — but even they can be enhanced through cyberspace.

At a minimum, between in-person meetings, members can continue discussions and conduct some business through email. But even better than that is taking advantage of the message boards that your friends at the Motley Fool will set up for your investment club — for free.

That's right. Imagine a common place where club members can post ideas and questions, where you can make announcements and agree on agendas. Stock ideas can be floated out and feedback solicited. Interim portfolio reports and meeting minutes can be shared. Late-breaking news about a stock your club owns can be discussed, as well.

A typical monthly club agenda has a lot of things on it. If your members all have online access, you can address a few of them on your message board, or at least get discussions underway. This can help you get more done and get it done more quickly. After all, there are 365 days in most years and your club will probably only meet on 12 of them. By communicating online, you can keep in touch on the remaining 353 days. After all, a lot can happen to your portfolio between meetings.

In addition to message boards, there are a lot of other resources available to investment clubs online. On the small chance that you're not aware of it already, the Motley Fool has a special area dedicated to investment clubs. You'll find it at:

http://www.fool.com/InvestmentClub

You can also use the Fool's website for stock research, for generating investment ideas, and for gathering information and opinions on a wide variety of companies and investment approaches.

Online Investment Clubs

Earlier in this primer, we urged you to take your investment club online and make the most of message board communication, among the other benefits of cyberspace. There's a way you can take even more advantage of the burgeoning online world, though. You can form or join an investment club that *only* meets online. This isn't for everyone. Consider the following points and issues:

A big advantage of online clubs is that you're not restricted by geography. If you'd really like to form a club with your childhood friends but they live in different corners of the earth, as long as you all have access to cyberspace it can be done. You're no longer limited to those people within driving distance.

With online clubs you're not even limited to people you know (or people your friends know). You could conceivably find a dozen fellow

Fools out on our message boards who strike you as smart and form a club with them — even if you all have never met. Indeed, ten years later, you might still have never met.

Remember, though, that there's a cloud to this silver lining. Be careful that you don't end up with a shady character among you. Out in the ether, it can be hard sometimes to tell who's a good guy and who's a rascal. (To minimize bad experiences, consider running credit checks on anyone who'll be handling money — you could also require dual signatures on outgoing checks or even get insurance in the form of a "fidelity bond," offered by the NAIC, among others.)

Online clubs can be effective for those with limited time or very busy schedules. If it seems difficult or impossible for you to attend regular meetings, you might still be able to manage a club that conducts its business via email or message boards. If you're not a social person, this is a good option, too.

Setting up an online club can be more difficult than setting up a traditional club. When you're meeting face-to-face, you can all review and sign any necessary paperwork in one fell swoop. Online clubs have to do it via the postal service. A good way is to send each member a copy of the required form and have them sign and return it — this is more effective than trying to pass one form from member to member.

It can be hard to maintain interest in an online investment club. Indeed, it can even be hard to tell when some members have lost interest. Be extra vigilant. Building a website for your club and engaging in occasional trivia (or other) games can be helpful, as well.

All-Women Clubs vs. All-Men Clubs

It's stereotype time. Which gender has traditionally been more cautious in matters financial and more hesitant and nervous about plunging into the world of investing in stocks? You guessed it — women. Despite this, the number of women investors has been rising rapidly. Consider these results from a 1997 survey commissioned by the Nasdaq stock market and a 1990 New York Stock Exchange survey: Whereas only 37% of investors in 1990 were female, that number had risen to 47% by 1997, and 45% of the female investors surveyed said that they're the primary investment decision-maker in their households.

The National Association of Investors Corp. (NAIC) has its own set of interesting statistics. Between 1960 and 1996, the percentage of NAIC member clubs that were all-women skyrocketed from 10% to 50%. When you consider that some clubs are men only and others are mixed, this means that the majority of all NAIC member clubs is all-women. In fact, three out of four new clubs formed are all-women clubs.

This speaks volumes. Women are increasingly interested in investing and are turning to clubs as a way to learn and invest. The NAIC reports that the number one goal of all-women clubs, ahead of turning a profit, is to learn about investing. They may do this out of genuine curiosity and a burning desire to learn — or because they realize that it's vitally important for them to be able to tend to their own or their family's finances. After all, according to a recent Bureau of the Census survey, 75% of the elderly poor in America are women.

You might now be depressed, thinking of all these damsels in financial distress. But the good news is that they don't necessarily need anyone to rescue them. Consider this last factoid: According to a 1995 NAIC study, all-women clubs have outperformed clubs composed of all men. How can this be? Well (warning: more stereotyping ahead), some speculate that while men are more apt to hear and rashly act on a hot stock tip from an acquaintance, women approach investing much more cautiously, wanting to think things through thoroughly and, if possible, discuss decisions with others.

The point we want to make is simply that while many women are often nervous about delving into financial matters, they shouldn't be. And investment clubs are an outstanding way for them to begin learning and doing.

So Fool on, sisters!

Faux Investment Clubs

Huh? What's a faux investment club? Well, it's just partly an investment club. We present this as one more option available to folks interested in forming an investment club. Basically, with a faux investment club, you form it just as you would a regular investment club — except you skip all the boring, confusing, or scary legal agreements. (Sound good? Keep reading.) This club operates just like a regular club, too, except you skip the little detail of collecting money and jointly investing it.

That's right. With the faux investment club, you pool resources like time and brainpower. And you research, present, and discuss various companies. But you stop there. You don't formally invest your money together. Instead, you just go home from the meeting and, based on information from the meeting, you decide what stock(s), if any, you'll buy for your personal portfolio.

The advantage with this kind of club is that there's no paperwork and no complicated accounting. If you ever disagree with the club's consensus regarding a stock, your finances won't be caught up in that decision.

There's a drawback, though. If you're not actually collecting and jointly investing money, members may not take their responsibilities as seriously. Without having actual money on the line — the money of others, to boot — the club might not operate as effectively.

It's up to you whether you pursue this option, but we wanted to make sure you considered it.

Words of Warning

Investment clubs, like almost anything else on earth, are not without some perils. Lest any Fool be caught off guard, we offer some words of warning below.

The Pitfall of the Pernicious Co-Member

Know that people you meet online or offline may not always be what they seem. This is far from merely a hazard of cyberspace — it's even been known to happen among friends. There's always a chance that you'll end up with a dastardly, unscrupulous person in your investment club. This is why, if your club is one that pools money and invests jointly, it's important to set up the club formally. Don't neglect to draft legal agreements and bylaws. Take some precautions. Perhaps set up your systems so that two people have to sign off on any financial transactions. This is important even if your club consists of only family members.

The Danger of Under-Delegation

This danger might seem less terrifying than the last one, but experienced investment club members have asked us to stress it. As one Fool noted: "Delegate, delegate, delegate... or you will be stuck with most of the work." Take note of your group's dynamics and make sure that the work is being shared by all. Anyone who isn't contributing his or her fair share may be enjoying a free ride and/or may be losing interest because they're not very involved. Anyone who's taking on too much may come to resent other club members and may burn out. Some might be reluctant to volunteer because they're not confident of their stock-researching abilities. Help these folks learn. It's in everyone's best interest to get all members up to speed so that all can contribute.

The Entanglement of Ennui

Over time, members might start to lose interest. This can be especially true if the market has been rising relentlessly (causing people to doubt the need for a club when it seems that any monkey can succeed in investing) or falling relentlessly (causing people to think that successful investing is impossible). It can be due to a club sticking to the same routine for several years without injecting anything new. Keep your club alive. Take the pulse of your members (figuratively). Are they still excited to be in the club? Do you all need a field trip or guest speaker to liven things up? If you ever feel your club is in trouble, tap the experience and counsel of others in our "Investment Clubs" message folder.

The Snare of Subterfuge

A club that isn't paying attention might find itself derailed by a member who's veered off toward unsound investing principles. Be vigilant. If a member is all excited about some article that sings the glories of technical investing or a friend's enthusiasm over a particular penny stock, be careful. Stick to the fundamentals, such as a company's earnings, growth, competition, and future. Otherwise, you might wake up one morning and find that your club's portfolio has half its funds invested in South American gold-mining ventures!

The Booby Trap of Time

Investment clubs take time. Make sure that you and your fellow members have the time to devote to it and are willing to devote that time. If you figure about one to three hours for a monthly meeting and two to four hours of research or work preparing for the meeting, that comes to three to seven hours that you'll have to commit each month. Broken up, it could be two or fewer hours per week. This is probably manageable for most people, but make sure that everyone has clear expectations.

If this still sounds like a lot of time, consider the alternative. If you want to invest successfully, you're still going to have to spend some time researching stocks and following companies you've invested in. For many people, participating in an investment club isn't adding significantly to the amount of work they'd do anyway. Remember that you also reap the benefit of the hours of work of many other club members.

The Menace of Math

This may seem obvious and silly, but make sure that you're performing your math calculations correctly. An incredible example of what we mean by this is provided by none other than the Beardstown Ladies. Apparently, their impressive 20-something-percent average annual return was kind of… wrong. It seems that a data input error caused them to overstate their returns. Fear not, though. This doesn't have to happen to you. Use specially designed software to help with your club's accounting and record keeping. Even without software, if you take the time to make sure that your record-keeping systems are sound, you should do fine.

It's true — there is math involved in investing. But it's all pretty much just good old addition, subtraction, multiplication, division, and percentages. Calculus, trigonometry, and logarithms are not required.

The Hazard of Humorlessness

Keep things fun, fellow Fools! Remember the words of that great investor of yore, Mary Poppins (if she invested, can you imagine her being anything but great at it?): "A spoonful of sugar helps the medicine go down." Learning about investing isn't as bad as swallowing some bitter tonic, but it's sure easier to do when you're having a good time. Never think that a sense of humor detracts from sound investing. If you ever find yourself forgetting this rule, check out some of Warren Buffett's enlightening and amusing annual letters to his shareholders — available online at:

http://www.berkshirehathaway.com/letters/letters.html

The Jeopardy of Jelly Donuts

Club members can tire of the same snacks each month. Try new treats. Perhaps refreshment duties should be rotated among all members. Don't let your fellow members fall into a "not-jelly-donuts-again" stupor.

In the spirit of the Beardstown Ladies books, we hereby offer the following recipes for snacks:

> **Cookies**
> Ingredients:
> 1 or more packages of cookies
>
> Preheat house to room temperature. Keep cookies in house until club meeting. Take cookies to club meeting. Open package(s). Arrange cookies on dish. Serve.

> **Pizza**
> Ingredients:
> 1 phone book
>
> Open phone book to yellow pages. Look under "pizza." Select pizza vendor with most amusing name, pizza vendor closest to you, or your favorite pizza vendor. Call and order pizza. Shake down fellow club members for cash. Pay delivery person when pizza arrives.

Popcorn

Ingredients:
Several packages microwave popcorn

Insert a package into the microwave. Set it to cook for the required amount of time. When you smell something unpleasant or when the smoke detector goes off, push "Stop." Remove and discard popcorn. Insert next package into microwave. Set it to cook for a shorter period. If it also turns into a crunchy brown mass, discard it and move on to the third package. Repeat until popcorn comes out fluffy and tasty. Do not — repeat, do not — try to extend the cooking time in order to pop those last few kernels. (This last point has been learned through many mistakes made in Fool HQ's own kitchen.)

General Foolish Investing

If you're going to be part of a Foolish Investment Club, you want to make sure you're being Foolish with your hard-earned wampum. Here's a quick overview of what we think is Foolish (good) and foolish (to be avoided).

What We Avoid

We steer clear of strategies that are more for speculators than investors, such as options, futures, penny stocks, day-trading, and technical analysis. They're great ways to end up losing most of your money — and in some cases, *more than all* of your money.

Speculators are out there trying to get lucky. You'll frequently hear them bandy about gambling terms: "I'm betting that the auto industry is going to turn around next month." "I'm taking a flier on stock XYZ — it should double soon." At the opposite end of the spectrum from speculators are investors. Investors are not looking to make a quick buck buying and selling whatever seems good at the moment. Investors instead carefully choose businesses that they want to own, and they hold on for as long as the situation remains compelling.

Technical Analysis. Technical analysis focuses on charts and graphs of a stock's past performance. Its proponents have devised an occult science of looking for patterns in these numbers. This approach largely ignores important concerns such as a company's business model, its competitive environment, and its prospects for growth. Technical analysis is really a short-term approach that focuses on the psychology of the market participants, guessing what investors will do next.

Options. Options are not necessarily reckless, but they're really only buying you time. When you buy a stock you own a part of a real company. With an option, you own the right to buy the stock — a right that is only valuable under certain conditions and that usually expires in a relatively short period. The option could be for the stock of a great company, but if things don't go your way within a short period of time, you're out of luck. Most options expire unexercised — that means that the people who bought or sold them didn't profit as they hoped they would.

Futures and Investing on Margin. Futures are even more dangerous, as you can lose more than the money you invest. The same thing can happen if you invest on margin aggressively.

Using margin means that you're essentially borrowing investing moolah from your broker. The loan is secured by the stocks that you own — they're your collateral. In a falling market, if the value of your collateral falls enough, you'll be served a "margin call," requiring you to either sell some stocks at low prices or infuse the account with additional cash. Fools can invest successfully using a little margin, but maxing out on it is fraught with peril.

Penny Stocks. Penny stocks are another mistake that many new investors make. Don't let your club fall prey to the misplaced appeal of a penny stock. A stock selling for 20 cents per share might seem like a screaming bargain, but ask yourself how it got to be priced so low. Most penny stocks are cheap for a reason. In addition, the price bears little relation to the value of the company. Remember: a stock priced at $200 per share might be much more of a bargain than one trading for a single dollar.

You might think about penny stocks this way... imagine each share of stock as a piece of pie. A 20-cent piece of pie might sound good, but it depends on how big the piece is, what kind of pie it is, and what condition it's in. It's better to spend more on a fresh and tasty big piece of apple pie than on a tiny ort of five-week-old cantaloupe pie. Focus on the quality and growth prospects of a company, not its stock price.

What We Embrace

The most direct way to learn Foolish investing is to read our "13 Steps to Investing Foolishly." These will be issued as a primer in the near future and are always accessible (free) on our website.

You can also learn more about the Foolish way of looking at and thinking about money by exploring our website and by reading our books. Foolish investing tenets will serve you well as an individual investor and also as a member of an investment club. Below are some guidelines. We have a lot more information available on these topics online. See the "Resources" section in the Appendix for details.

First, make sure no club member is suffering from serious credit card debt. Such debt should be paid off before anyone begins investing — otherwise you end up digging a hole when you're trying to build a mountain.

Make sure your group has defined some reasonable expectations for performance and that it establishes procedures for tracking results. We like to compare our performance with the S&P 500 Index, which is a bundle of 500 of America's biggest and brightest companies.

Consider using a discount brokerage instead of a full-service brokerage. Traditionally, full-service brokerages charge high commissions because they're not only executing trades for you, but also recommending what you should buy and sell. Foolish investors learn to make their own decisions. Since they don't need "professional" advice, they can enjoy significantly lower commissions.

Consider plunking early dollars into an S&P 500 index fund until your group is comfortable moving on to more advanced investing. This type of mutual fund has topped the vast majority of its brethren, chalking up 10% to 11% average annual returns over the past several decades.

Consider making the Dow Dividend Approach a cornerstone of your group's portfolio. There are many variations of this approach, including the Foolish Four, and they've returned, on average, between 16% and 20% per year. The basic idea is that you use a simple system that zeroes in on stocks among the 30 in the Dow Jones Industrial Average that are beaten down and poised to rebound. This is an easy way to keep four or five solid companies in your club portfolio — without even having to research them!

Once your group is comfortable researching stocks and you're ready to pick some in which to invest, the best place to start might be large-cap companies. These are the big, established firms like Procter & Gamble, Sears, Boeing, and so on. Once you have a few of these in your portfolio, you can move on to some small-cap stocks. These are usually younger companies that have the potential to grow more rapidly than large-caps but are also more risky. Small-caps might include specialty retailers, small-but-growing restaurant chains, and young high-tech firms.

When you're researching stocks, don't rely just on P/E ratios or a stock's price trends. There are a few Foolish stock valuation techniques described in this primer, and you'll find more methods outlined on our website and in various other Fool publications.

Experienced investment clubs can consider shorting stock, where you try to profit from stocks that you expect to drop in price. Understand that this kind of investing requires more attention. You don't want the stock to move too far in the wrong direction between club meetings. When shorting stocks, your group should have a clear idea of the price at which you'll close out the short position and you should have a mechanism in place to get out mid-month, if necessary.

A Bunch of Eggs, a Bunch of Baskets

As your club adds stocks to its portfolio, you should make sure that your holdings are diversified. As the old saying goes, you don't want all your eggs in one basket.

You might feel diversified if you have eight different stocks. But if they're Dell Computer, IBM, Compaq Computer, Gateway 2000, Apple Computer, Microsoft, Intel, and Hewlett-Packard, that's not diversified at all. They're all related to the personal computer industry. If for some reason computers are replaced by something else, or if computers just plummet in price for some reason, your portfolio will be in serious trouble.

Aim to be diversified on several fronts — industry, company size, and number of stocks held. Spread your stocks across different industries, such as food, banks, software, aerospace, apparel, retailing, construction, drugs, healthcare, insurance, recreation, oil & gas, publishing, and so on. Have a balance between large-cap companies (like General Electric and Microsoft), medium-cap companies (like La Quinta Inns and Papa John's International) and small-cap and micro-cap companies (like Sharper Image Corp. and Quigley Corporation).

Of course, there's such a thing as over-diversification. Most mutual funds suffer from this. If you hold 100 stocks and one of them quadruples, it's not going to make much of a difference in your bottom line. We recommend that portfolios hold between eight and fifteen stocks.

A final consideration is weighting. If your portfolio has ten stocks but one of them skyrockets so much that it now represents 50% of the value of your whole portfolio, you might consider selling some of the shares. We'd rather not see more than 33% of our portfolio's value in a single stock, because if something unpleasant happens to that one stock, it will have a *big* effect.

No investment club primer would be complete without some discussion of stock picking and valuation methods. After you've gotten the club together, done all the boring paperwork, and had a few meetings, everyone will probably be excited to buy the first stock. We can help a bit in that department.

Learning how to pick stocks isn't something you can do in an hour or a day. It's really a life-long pursuit. In fact, there's no way to really do the subject justice in the limited space we have here. Please use this guide as a starting point in your studies, and then come online with us at the Motley Fool and learn more and more each day.

One other thing to understand is that you will absolutely make mistakes and lose money on stocks in your investment club portfolio. It's going to happen, so be ready for it and don't despair. In fact, you may lose money on your very first pick, so hang in there if you do. One of the greatest benefits of belonging to a club is that you can help one another learn where you went wrong with a particular stock. Learning from mistakes and avoiding them in the future is critical to doing well.

Picking Stocks

A Starting Point: Your Best Friend

Most of us have a best friend who, over the years, has displayed certain traits that make them our closest pal. Maybe your friend is incredibly generous and a great listener. Perhaps she has a fantastic sense of humor and is very thoughtful. Just as there are certain characteristics that make someone a great friend, there are also certain characteristics that make companies great. Let's list just a few things that you might look for in a company:

1. Repeat purchase. Some of the greatest investments in the world have been in companies selling products that people buy again and again and again. You probably buy soup, soda pop, razor blades, and laundry detergent regularly, right? Well, you can buy stock in the companies that make all of these things. For example:

Campbell Soup (NYSE: CPB) has one of the best-known food brands in the world. Its brand names include Franco-American, Godiva chocolates, Prego, Pepperidge Farm, V8, and Pace.

Coca-Cola (NYSE: KO) is the largest maker of soft drinks in the world, with brand names such as Sprite, Minute Maid, Barq's, Fanta, Five Alive, Mello Yello, Surge, Bacardi, Hi-C, and Nestea.

Gillette (NYSE: G) is the world's largest maker of razor blades, including the incredibly popular Sensor line of shaving products. Its other brands include Duracell, Right Guard, Parker Pen, Paper Mate, Braun, Oral-B, Liquid Paper, and White Rain.

Procter & Gamble (NYSE: PG) is a global leader in products like laundry detergent, with popular brand names like Tide, Downy, and Cheer in its stable. Its non-detergent brands include Pampers, Bounty, Pert, Tampax, Clearasil, Ivory, Max Factor, Oil of Olay, Old Spice, Crisco, Duncan Hines, Folgers, Pringles, Nyquil, Scope, and Crest.

If your club had invested an equal amount in each of these companies at the start of this decade, you would easily have outperformed the market indices.

2. Great Past Performance. We often hear on television commercials that "past performance is not an indication of future results." In many of his speaking engagements, our cofounder David Gardner says, "This is one of the greatest myths out there. Past performance is almost always an indication of future results." Think about it. If a company has been kicking butt for the past five years, chances are it's been doing something very well. Perhaps this company is worth looking at. (Note that this advice is less applicable to mutual funds and other investments. We're talking here about individual companies with great long-term records.)

When evaluating a company's historical performance, how far back should you look? Five years is a reasonable range of time, but feel free to go back a little farther if you're so inclined. Look for growing sales and earnings, among other things.

Should an appealing company have a poor track record, you don't have to automatically rule it out. After all, past performance isn't the only factor to consider when evaluating a company. Find out *why* it has performed poorly — perhaps the company has set itself up for a turnaround.

3. Strong Brand Name. Many books teach you to "invest in what you know." This is fantastic advice — although we might temper it a mite and recommend that you "research and then invest in what you know." Most of the things we purchase in our everyday lives are made by companies that trade in the stock market. You can buy stock in Tootsie Roll, Nike, Dell Computer, PepsiCo, Microsoft, Sara Lee, etc. All of these companies are household names and, in some cases, their products have actually become part of our language. For example, we rarely say, "Got a facial tissue?" — instead, you're more likely to hear, "Got some Kleenex?" Kleenex, like Xerox, is a brand name that is so familiar that it has actually become incorporated into the language. Look for companies that are a part of your life and that have strong brand-name recognition.

There are many other characteristics to look for in potential "buy" candidates, but these are three good ones to start with. If you find companies that have all three traits, you may be on your way to finding a new best friend.

Gathering Information

Once you have a few good ideas, it's time to look even deeper. Even companies that appear to be winners can sometimes have problems below the surface that we don't see right away. How many times have you heard something awful about a neighbor, only to think, "Wow — I had no idea." Unfortunately, that sometimes holds true for companies, too. You need to take a close look at a company's business.

If you're assigned to research a company for your club, you should get its phone number. Actually, you should get a few phone numbers. Remember that for any single company, you should also investigate a few of its peers in the same industry, to give you a frame of reference for comparisons.

To find a company's phone number, try checking the Motley Fool's message folder for the stock. On the Motley fool website you can use the "Company Snapshot" feature located in the quotes and news area to find phone numbers (and lots of other useful information). Many local libraries carry *Value Line* or Standard & Poor's stock reports, which include company phone numbers. Or call the stock exchange where the stock trades. Most American companies trade on one of the following three exchanges. You can call and ask for the phone number of any company.

Stock Exchange Phone Numbers

American Stock Exchange	(212) 306-1490
The Nasdaq Stock Market:	(202) 728-8039
New York Stock Exchange:	(212) 656-5060

Give each company a call, ask for the Investor Relations department, and then ask them to send you an "investor's information package." (It's free!) Here's what it should contain (you might want to specify on the phone exactly what you're expecting to receive):

What You Want In An Investor Packet

1. The most recent Annual Report
2. The most recent 10-K
3. The most recent 10-Q
4. All recent press releases
5. All available analyst reports

Annual reports and 10-K reports are issued once a year. Every three months, 10-Q reports are filed. Once you own stock in a company, most of these reports and earnings press releases should be sent to you automatically — if they're not, ask your broker what's up, or just call the company and ask to be put on its mailing list.

In the months between annual reports, you'll find a company's most recent financial numbers in the latest 10-Q report. These reports contain the three main financial statements that each publicly traded company is required to provide: the balance sheet, the statement of operations (a.k.a. the income statement or profit and loss statement), and the statement of cash flows.

Once the packages arrive, it's time to do a little detective work.

Digging Deeper

Understanding how companies operate is very similar to understanding how your own personal finances operate. Thinking about your own principles and ideals can help you understand how to evaluate a company. Below are some things to look for in a company's financial statements. They'll probably strike you as common sense.

1. Little or No Debt. Clearly, we'd all like to be debt-free. Nobody likes paying credit card bills or making car payments. The same holds true for great investments. You should look for companies that have little or no debt as a percentage of their total equity. You can find both of these numbers in a company's *balance sheet*. In the section under "Liabilities and Shareholder's Equity," you'll find both debt and equity numbers. All you have to do is compare the numbers to one another.

Computing the Debt-to-Equity Ratio

If XYZ Company has $1 million in long-term debt and $10 million in shareholder's equity, the debt is 10% of equity. (1 divided by 10 equals 0.10, or 10%.) In growth companies, more than 20% debt is not desirable.

2. Rising Sales and Earnings. You also want to buy companies that are growing their sales (revenues), as well as their earnings (net income). When comparing your own personal circumstances to that of a company, your annual salary is like a company's sales and your savings are like a company's net income. After you deduct taxes and all of your expenses out of your annual salary, you have money left over (we hope!). This would be your savings. For a company, after it deducts its cost of goods sold and then deducts taxes and other expenses, it's left with its bottom-line savings, or net income. You can find these numbers by looking at the *income statement*.

You want to find a company that is increasing its sales and net income each year, just as you'd like to increase your salary and savings each year. Just how much is enough growth? Ask 20 people and you'll probably get 20 different answers.

Foolish Growth Target

We think, as a general rule, that an annual average of 20% growth in sales and earnings is outstanding. Sometimes you can do well with companies growing more slowly than that, but 20% is a good target.

3. Enough Cash in the Bank. Have you ever been advised to have six months' worth of expenses saved in the bank in case something bad happens and you're out of work? This is meant to be a little war chest in case you fall on hard times, right? After all, you need to be able to pay bills if things get sticky. Well, the same thing applies for your favorite company. It should have at least enough cash or short-term investments on hand to be able to pay all bills coming due.

Enough Cash on Hand?
The Current Ratio

This is really easy to figure out. All you have to do is look at the balance sheet again and compare "Current Assets" to "Current Liabilities."

If Current Assets are larger than Current Liabilities, the company has enough money to handle its short-term needs. If not, be careful. It may end up having to borrow money to pay off its debts.

To evaluate this, investors often calculate something called the "Current Ratio," which divides Current Assets by Current Liabilities. If the ratio is less than 1.0, the company doesn't have the assets to cover liabilities.

You want the current ratio to be above 1.0, but not astronomically high. A very high number means that the company is letting piles of money sit around instead of using them.

These are just a few of the things that you can and should look for when examining a company. There are many, many more that you can learn about by joining us at www.fool.com.

A Company's Price Tag

After finding a great company and checking out its financial statements, the last question you have to ask yourself is whether it's too expensive, fairly priced, or a bargain. Trying to determine if a company's stock is a good value is one of the most difficult things for an investor to do.

We can't fully do justice to stock valuation in this primer, but we don't want to send you home without some lovely parting gifts. In the sections below we'll introduce a few handy valuation measures. These are but a few of the many tools that should be in every Fool's toolbox.

It's very useful to calculate numbers like the ones below for the company you're interested in as well as for some peer companies in its industry. This way, you can compare them and see which one is more attractive.

Here's an important point to mull over, though. As we all know from our regular lives, sometimes the best things in life are among the most expensive. The best refrigerator usually has a high price tag. The highest performance car is also pretty expensive. Some have suggested that the same rules apply for the stock market. It has been argued that the best companies are always expensive and that if you wait for them to get "cheap," you'll be waiting forever. This is something to think about.

On to some valuation measures!

The Price-to-Earnings (P/E) Ratio

We all see P/E ratios in newspaper stock listings. It is one of the most common valuation yardsticks that investors use.

The P/E is a company's current share price divided by its earnings per share (EPS). The EPS used is usually from the last year (trailing four quarters), but can also be calculated using the EPS estimates for the upcoming year. Companies include EPS numbers in their earnings press releases and in their 10-Q reports (on the income statement).

EPS is calculated by simply dividing the dollar amount of the earnings a company reports by the number of shares it currently has outstanding. Thus, if XYZ Corp. has one million shares outstanding and has earned one million dollars in the past 12 months, it has a trailing EPS of $1.00. (Trailing EPS looks at the last four quarters reported, which are not necessarily the four quarters covered in the most recent annual report. The annual report might have come out ten months ago, so the four quarters it covers are even farther back.)

Calculating Earnings Per Share (EPS)

$$\frac{\$1,000,000 \text{ earnings}}{1,000,000 \text{ shares}} = \$1.00 \text{ EPS}$$

The earnings per share alone means absolutely nothing, though. To get some context, you have to compare the earnings to something like the stock price, which is what the P/E ratio does. The P/E ratio takes the stock price and divides it by the last four quarters' earnings. For instance if, in our example above, XYZ Corp. was trading at $15 per share, it would have a P/E of 15.

Calculating Price-to-Earnings (P/E) Ratio

$$\frac{\$15 \text{ share price}}{\$1.00 \text{ in trailing 12-mo. EPS}} = 15 \text{ P/E}$$

Many investors seek companies with low P/E ratios, as this can indicate beaten-down companies likely to rebound. Low P/Es might be attractive, but understand that P/Es vary by industry. Automobile companies and banks typically sport low P/Es, while software and Internet-related companies command higher ones. Don't compare kumquats to kiwis.

Once you have a handle on the P/E ratio, you'll probably want to start comparing it to something. That's what the Fool Ratio does.

The Fool Ratio (PEG Ratio)

The Fool Ratio is based on a simple premise: In a fully and fairly valued situation, a growth stock's price-to-earnings (P/E) ratio should equal the company's annual earnings growth rate. (This is why it's also called the PEG Ratio — for P/E to growth rate.)

Fool Ratios above 1.50 scare us, while those 0.50 or lower attract us. A ratio of 0.50 suggests that earnings are growing twice as fast as the stock price, and that the stock is trading at half its fair value. Such a company

Calculating the Fool Ratio (PEG Ratio)

When the P/E and the growth rate are equal, the Fool Ratio is 1.00 and suggests a fairly priced stock. Ratios under 1.00 suggest under-valued stocks, while ratios greater than 1.00 suggest overvaluation.

If Computer Game Rehabilitation Services Inc. has a P/E ratio of 30 and its earnings are growing at 60% annually, you would divide 30 by 60 and get an appealing 0.50 Fool Ratio.

Meanwhile, if Pong Inc. has a P/E ratio of 11 and is growing at 6%, its Fool Ratio is 1.83 (11 divided by 6 = 1.83). By this measure, the stock price appears steep.

would be a prime candidate for further research. (Never just buy a stock based on any single valuation metric.)

You can often just eyeball a few numbers and get a good general impression of the Fool Ratio. For example, if a company is growing earnings at 18% per year, a fair P/E ratio for it would be 18. If the P/E is a lot lower, that suggests an attractive valuation. If it's higher, the stock price might have gotten ahead of itself.

Nifty though it may be, the Fool Ratio should serve as a general guide rather than a precise instrument. Remember that it focuses on earnings and doesn't take into account important factors such as debt, cash, amortization, depreciation, and the full merits and shortcomings of a company's business. It also doesn't work with cyclical, financial, unprofitable, or large and established companies. It is best used for growth companies with annual sales under $1 billion, not companies like Sears, General Motors, or Exxon.

The Price-to-Sales Ratio (PSR)

The P/E ratio compares a company's stock price to its earnings, but what if there are no earnings? Well, then you can compare the stock price to sales (also called revenues). Every time a company sells a customer a product or service, it is generating revenues. Whether or not a company has made money in the last year, there are always revenues. Revenue-based valuations are achieved using the price-to-sales ratio, often simply abbreviated PSR. (This handy measure works for all kinds of companies — not just unprofitable ones.)

The price-to-sales ratio takes the current market capitalization of a company and divides it by the last 12 months' revenues. The market capitalization is the current price at which the market is valuing the company, arrived at by multiplying the current share price times the number of shares outstanding. For instance, if Lord-of-the-Trance Hypnotics Inc. has ten million shares outstanding, priced at $10 a share, then the market capitalization is $100 million.

Some investors are even more conservative and add the current long-term debt of the company to the total current market value of its stock to get the market capitalization. The logic here is that if you were to acquire the company, you would acquire its debt as well, effectively paying that much more. This avoids problems like comparing PSRs between two companies where one has taken out enormous debt that it has used to boost sales and the other is debt-free but has lower sales.

Calculating the Price-to-Sales Ratio (PSR)

(Regular) Market Capitalization = Shares Outstanding * Current Share Price

(Conservative) Market Capitalization = (Shares Outstanding * Current Share Price) + Current Long-term Debt

The next step in calculating the PSR is to add up the revenues from the last four quarters and divide this number into the market capitalization.

Say Lord-of-the-Trance had $200 million in sales over the last four quarters and currently has no long-term debt. The PSR would be:

$$\frac{(10,000,000 \text{ shares} * \$10/\text{share}) + \$0 \text{ debt}}{\$200 \text{ million revenues}}$$

$$= \frac{100,000,000}{200,000,000} = 0.5 \text{ PSR}$$

Companies often consider the PSR when making an acquisition. If you have ever read about a deal being done based on a certain "multiple to sales," you have seen the PSR in use. As this is a perfectly legitimate way for a company to value an acquisition, many simply transfer it to the stock market and use it to value a company as an ongoing concern.

In general, the lower the PSR, the better. PSR ranges vary by industry, though, so make sure to compare a company with its peers. The PSR is also related to a company's growth rate — rapidly growing firms can justify higher PSRs. Noted investor Ken Fisher, famous for using the PSR to value stocks, looks for companies with PSRs below 1.0 to find value stocks the market might currently be overlooking. This is the most common application of the PSR and is actually a pretty good indicator of value, according to the research done by James O'Shaughnessey.

The PSR is also handy when a company has not made money in the last year. Unless the corporation is going out of business, the PSR can tell you whether its sales are being valued at a discount to its peers. Assume that Lord-of-the-Trance lost money in the past year, but has a PSR of 0.50 while many companies in the same industry have PSRs of 2.0 or higher. If it can turn itself around and start making money again, it is likely to have substantial upside as it increases that PSR to be more in line with its peers. There are some years during recessions, for example, when none of the auto companies make money. Does this mean they are all worthless and there is no way to compare them? Not at all. You just need to use the PSR instead of the P/E and measure how much you are paying for a dollar of sales instead of a dollar of earnings.

Keep in Touch!

There's much more to talk about regarding stock picking, stock valuation, and portfolio building. We hope that each of you will bring your investing club online and learn with us each day. We'll be looking for you on our website!

We're sure that despite our best efforts, this primer has not answered every question you might have about starting and running an investment club. We doubt that any book could answer every question for every kind of club.

But you're in luck! Your experience of learning about Foolish investment clubs doesn't have to end here. We've got a hustling, bustling online area to support this modest literary endeavor.

Come to www.fool.com and drop by the message folders in our online Investment Club area. There you can read the thoughts and experiences of others who have formed clubs or who are considering doing so. You can ask and answer questions and learn from fellow Fools.

Even if you don't have questions, we'd love to hear from you. We'd like to learn more about your club's doings, so that the materials we develop for investment clubs incorporate your experiences, ideas, tips, and thoughts. (We might even ask your club to try out some new products being developed by the mad scientists at FoolLabs.) Post your thoughts online and share your discoveries and experience with others, or send us an email at InvClub@fool.com.

Fool on!

A Glossary
for Beginning
Investors

Analyst: A financial professional who analyzes securities to determine a "fair value" or "intrinsic value" for those securities. The term is generally applied to almost any professional investor who does research of some kind. There is no specific degree or certification required to be called an analyst.

Annual Report: A yearly statement of a public company's operating and financial performance, often punctuated with pictures of families enjoying the firm's products and/or services.

Appreciation: Increase in the price (or value) of a stock or other asset. Appreciation is one component of total return.

Balance Sheet: An important financial report regularly issued by companies. It provides a look at a company's assets, debts, and shareholder equity at one particular point in time. What's so balanced about it? Well, assets are set equal to debt and shareholder equity. So if a company has no liabilities, its shareholder equity is equal to its assets. A company with a lot of liabilities will have little shareholder equity.

Bear: So you think that the market is headed south? You're bracing yourself for a crash or correction? You feel that stock XYZ will soon be taking a tumble? Guess what — you're a bear! Bears are investors with pessimistic outlooks, as opposed to "Bulls."

Blue-chip Stocks: Blue-chip stocks are those of companies that are the most well-known and well-trusted. These companies are usually very large and often very old, such as IBM, AT&T, and Texaco. All of the Dow 30 stocks are considered blue chips.

Bonds: Bonds essentially represent loans to companies or governments. If you buy a bond, you are lending money to the issuer, and you will usually collect some regular interest payments until your money is returned to you.

Brokers: Stockbrokers are agents who buy or sell stocks for the public.

Bull: Are your glasses rose-colored? Do you see nothing but blue skies ahead for the stock market or a particular security? Then you're a bull — an optimistic investor — as opposed to a "bear."

Capital: A business's cash or property, or an investor's pile of cash.

Capital Gain: You bought a stock and later sold it. If you made a profit, that's your capital gain. If you lost money, it's a capital loss.

Chief Executive Officer (CEO): The CEO is the highest executive officer in a corporation, sort of like the captain of a ship. He or she is accountable to the company's Board of Directors and is frequently a member of that Board. The CEO participates in setting strategy with the Board and other officers and is responsible for the tactics in meeting the corporation's goals.

Cold Call: It's cold because the person doesn't know you from a snow-drift. To build business, many new brokers must call people they don't know and try to sell an investment idea or their services as a broker.

Commission: Whenever you buy or sell shares of stock, your broker will charge a commission (sales fee). Commissions vary greatly in size and can make trading very expensive if you are only buying or selling small numbers of shares.

Compounding: Compounding is when your money increases regularly and when the amount it increases by also increases. For example, if you have $100 growing at 10% per year, it will be $110 in one year (having increased by $10), and then $121 in the second year (having increased by $11), and $133 in the third year (having increased by $12). Over large periods of time, compounding can make money grow tremendously.

Correction: If you hear someone talk about a "correction," she means a drop in the market. A big correction is a crash. The word correction is used because people think that sometimes the market has grown more than it should, so it is due to be corrected. Any time that commentators cannot find a reason for an individual stock or the entire market falling, they call it a correction.

Crash: A market crash is a big correction. It is what many investors always worry about. The stock market never goes up in a straight line, so there will always be crashes and corrections. It can take a few days, months, or years for a market to recover after a crash.

Day Trader: Day traders are in and out of the market many times during the course of one trading session and often do not hold a position in any security overnight. This approach tends to generate a lot of expenses in the form of commissions and denies the day trader the ability to participate in the long-term creation of wealth through compounding that is possible if you own shares of a quality business.

Discount Broker: Brokers who offer fewer of the "services" championed by full-service brokers, but charge cheaper fees and commissions. Discount brokers are ideal for do-it-yourselfer investors (you!). (Also see Broker and Full-Service Broker.)

Diversification: If you're keeping all your eggs in one basket, you're not diversified. Good investors divide their money among roughly 8-15 stocks, so if anything terrible happens to one company, they won't lose too much. You also want to diversify your holdings over different industries.

Dividend: A distribution from a company to a stockholder in the form of cash, shares of stock, or other assets. The most common kind of dividend is a distribution of earnings.

Dividend Yield: The income relative to the current share price that a company pays out to shareholders as a dividend, usually expressed in percentage terms.

Dividend Reinvestment Plan (DRP): Dividend Reinvestment Plans allow you to buy shares of stock directly from companies, bypassing brokers and broker commissions. With DRPs, you usually have to own at least one share of the stock before enrolling in the program. A new variation of DRPs, Direct Stock Purchase plans, permit you to buy even your first share directly from the company. Hundreds of major companies offer these plans.

Dow, or Dow Jones Industrial Average: The 30 companies chosen by editors of Dow Jones & Company that are supposed to epitomize the very best American corporations and reflect the landscape of corporate America. TV news announcers often report on how "the Dow" did during the day.

Dow Dividend Approach (DDA): This approach has beaten the market averages over a number of decades. It's also called the "Dogs of the Dow" because one buys the highest-yielding stocks in the Dow Jones Industrial Average, which usually implies that they've been beaten down. The approach has been successful because the Dow companies are firms that are solid financially and have successful business models; the decline in their share prices is usually temporary.

Earnings: The money a company puts in the bank after all of the costs of delivering a product or service have been accounted for. (Also see Revenues.)

Earnings Per Share (EPS): Net income (earnings or profits) divided by the current number of common shares of stock outstanding. This is one of the principal elements used in determining at what value the shares should trade.

Equities: Another way of referring to stock. Because they represent a proportional share in the business, they are equitable claims on the business itself.

Fair Value: The theoretical price at which a company is "fairly valued," meaning that it would not be reasonable to assume that the shares will rise. Fair value at any given point is derived from a number of qualitative and quantitative aspects of the business.

Fool: Fools are investors who have learned enough about investing to take charge of their own financial futures, picking stocks on their own after researching the companies. Fools aim to outperform the market.

Full-Service Broker: Full-service brokers earn commissions for each trade made in a customer's account. They make *more* money by trading in and out of lots of investments. They are sometimes referred to as a "full-price brokers." (Also see Broker, Discount Broker and Stockbroker.)

Income: See Earnings

Index Fund: The only type of mutual fund that makes sense to us. While most mutual funds are actively (mis-)managed, index funds are generally computer-driven, designed to mimic the performance of a given stock market index such as the S&P 500. (Also see Standard & Poor's 500 Stock Index.)

Initial Public Offering (IPO): A company's first sale of stock to the public. To do an IPO, a company needs to use an underwriter. (Also see Underwriter.)

Margin: 1. Borrowing money to use specifically for buying securities of any kind in a brokerage account. 2. A measure of profitability of a company, such as profit margin, operating margin, or gross margin.

Market Capitalization: The total market value of a company. Market capitalization is calculated by multiplying a firm's share price by the number of shares outstanding.

Marmot: Any of a group of thick-bodied rodents.

Money Market: Money market funds put money in a bunch of short-term investments (i.e. bonds). If you invest your money in the money market, you'll usually earn a little more than the current interest rate offered by banks. This is a safe, but conservative, way to invest money.

The Motley Fool: The Motley Fool is dedicated to teaching people how to successfully invest in the stock market. The mission? To inform, amuse, and enrich.

Mutual Funds: Mutual funds are pooled amounts of money that are invested according to an established investment strategy. Presiding over a fund is a manager (or managers) responsible for achieving the fund's stated investment objective. (Also see Index Fund.) Most mutual funds underperform the market, but many people don't have the confidence or know-how to invest on their own, so they put their money in mutual funds.

Nasdaq Stock Market: A national stock market where trades are made exclusively via computers. The second-largest stock market in the country, the Nasdaq is home to many high-tech companies.

New York Stock Exchange (NYSE): The largest and oldest stock exchange in the United States. This Wall Street haunt is the one frequently featured on television, with hundreds of traders on the floor staring up at screens and answering phones, ready to trade stocks on-command from their firms.

Orangeade: A drink made with orange juice, water, and sugar.

P/E Ratio (Price-to-Earnings): A stock's price divided by its annual earnings per share is its P/E ratio. P/E ratios can suggest when a stock is over- or undervalued, but investors should look at much more than just a company's P/E ratio. P/E ratios are usually listed along with a stock's price in a newspaper's business section. Often, the higher the sustainable growth rate of a company, the higher its P/E ratio.

Penny Stocks: Penny stocks are low-priced or very risky stocks that usually trade for less than $5. Many years ago, when stock prices were lower, penny stocks traded for less than a dollar — that's how they got their name.

Portfolio: A collection of investments. For example, your investment portfolio might be made up of stock in a dozen different companies. Or it might have some bonds, some stocks, and a mutual fund.

Profits: See Income

Publicly Traded: If a company has shares trading on the market, it is said to be publicly traded. That means that whoever owns the shares owns the company. If you own 5% of the shares, you own 5% of the company. Companies "go public" in order to raise money. Many companies, like Levi Strauss, are privately held and not publicly traded.

Quarter: Roughly equal to three months, businesses have four quarters in every fiscal year for which they report their financial results. After each quarter, a company is required to file a 10-Q or 10-K report with the SEC, providing investors with juicy details on how the company is doing.

Return: The word "return" is used to describe the money you make on your investments. Savings accounts at banks, for example, offer low returns (they pay little in interest), while some stocks can offer spectacular returns (perhaps doubling your money).

Revenues (Sales): The money that a company collects from customers in payment for products or services. (Also see Earnings.)

Risk: Risk is often associated with return because to try and earn a high rate of return, you usually have to take on risk. The different ways you can invest your money vary in how risky they are. For example, bonds are usually less risky than stocks, but they offer lower returns.

S&P 500: See Standard and Poor's 500 Stock Index.

Standard and Poor's 500 Stock Index (S&P 500): An index of 500 of the biggest and best companies in American industry selected by an editorial board at Standard & Poor's. The index is often used as a proxy for the overall performance of the stock market and is often used as a way to measure how well mutual fund managers have performed relative to the market. If the companies, as a group, rise in price, the S&P 500 Index rises, as well.

Securities: A fancy name for shares of stock or bonds, "securities" is just a blanket way to refer to any kind of financial asset that can be traded.

Shareholder: You, if you own stock in a company. As a shareholder you get an invitation to the company's annual meeting, copies of financial reports, and you have the right to vote on the members of the Board of Directors and other company matters.

Shares Outstanding: The total number of shares of stock a company has outstanding.

Stock: Shares of publicly traded companies. A share of stock legally represents part of a corporation.

Stockbroker: An individual who has been licensed by the National Association of Securities Dealers to trade stocks and advise clients on various personal finance issues. Considered by many to be the fifth-oldest profession after prostitutes, pimps, tax collectors, and accountants. (Also see Broker.)

Ticker Symbol: All companies that are publicly traded have a ticker symbol for their shares. This is so that the company can be identified with just a few letters. Thanks to the ticker symbol, you don't have to say or write "Minnesota Mining and Manufacturing" — you can just say "MMM." Other examples of tickers are "Z" for Woolworth and "MSFT" for Microsoft.

Valuation: The determination of a fair value for a security. If you don't use some reasonable method, then you have what is technically called a "guess" or a "hope."

Wall Street: Also known as "the Street" in cocktail-party patter, this is the main drag in New York City's financial district, although the term is mostly used to refer to the establishment of investing "gooroos."

Appendix

Contents

Resources

The Motley Fool Website

The Motley Fool home page address:
http://www.fool.com

Investment Clubs:
http://www.fool.com/InvestmentClub

13 Steps to Investing Foolishly:
http://www.fool.com/School/13Steps/13Steps.htm

Debt:
http://www.fool.com/credit

Brokerages:
http://www.fool.com/media/DiscountBrokerageCenter/
DiscountBrokerageCenter.htm

The Dow Dividend Approach:
http://www.fool.com/DDow/DDExplained.htm

FoolMart:
http://www.foolmart.com

Some Books of Interest

The Motley Fool Investment Guide, by David and Tom Gardner

The Motley Fool Investment Workbook, by David and Tom Gardner

You Have More Than You Think, by David and Tom Gardner

Beating the Street, by Peter Lynch

Learn to Earn, by Peter Lynch

One Up on Wall Street, by Peter Lynch

Buffett: The Making of an American Capitalist, by Roger Lowenstein

Built to Last: Successful Habits of Visionary Companies, by James C. Collins & Jerry I. Porras

Starting and Running a Profitable Investment Club, by Thomas E. O'Hara and Kenneth S. Janke, Sr. of the National Association of Investors Corp.

Other Web Resources

National Association of Investors Corp.:
http://better-investing.org

Douglas Gerlach's Invest-O-Rama!
http://investorama.com/naic.html

Directory of Investment Clubs Online:
http://investorama.com/olclubs.shtml

Model Online Investment Club:
http://www.better-investing.org/molic/

NAIC Club Accounting Software:
http://www.better-investing.org/computer/nca.html

Other Resources

Investor's Business Daily is a good newspaper for investors. Visit its website at www.investors.com or call 1-800-831-2525 for a free two-week subscription. Included with the trial is a videotape on investing.

Industry Snapshot is the Motley Fool's industry overview that examines a different industry every two weeks. Each issue includes a look at an industry or industry segment, a review of some of its top players and their financials, and an investment idea. Available from FoolMart online or at the phone number below.

FoolMart, our store, will be happy to mail you a free catalog: 1-888-665-3665

Sample Investment Club Bylaws

Bylaws of Them Crazy Fools Investment Club
[Your name may vary]

A)   Duties of Partners

Annually, at the first meeting in February, partners shall elect the following Officers and assign duties as described below by a majority vote. [*These positions may be combined, or a club can have additional jobs.*] These officers shall serve for a term of one year.

1. President. The President shall preside over meetings, set meeting dates and locations, appoint committees, and see that resolutions passed by the partnership are carried out.

2. Vice President. The Vice President takes the place of the President when the Present is absent or incapacitated. The Vice President shall assign companies to report on at Club meetings to each partner and shall be responsible for insuring that the Club's study program is properly carried out.

3. Secretary. The Secretary shall keep a record of the actions authorized by the partners and notify partners of meetings and other activities.

4. Treasurer. The Treasurer shall keep a record of the Club's receipts and disbursements and partners' interests in the Club. The Treasurer will give partners receipts for payments and prepare the Club's monthly Valuation Statement in coordination with the Broker Liaison. She will see that the needed tax information is compiled and file the necessary reports.

5. Broker Liaison. The Broker Liaison shall place the buy and sell orders authorized by the partners with the Club's broker and help the Treasurer prepare the monthly Valuation Statement.

6. Snack Coordinator. The Snack Coordinator ensures that adequate supplies of snacks are provided for each meeting.

B)   Guests

Partners may invite guests to any meeting of the Club as long as advance clearance is obtained from the host of the meeting. When consideration is given to adding partners to the Club under paragraph 16 of the Club's partnership agreement, anyone considered shall have been a guest for at least two prior meetings.

C)   Meetings

The Club shall hold a meeting on the third Saturday of each month at a place designated by the Club. The Secretary shall give written notice of each meeting to each partner at least one week before the meeting. Special meetings may be called by the President upon similar notice to the other partners.

D)   Procedures

The monthly valuation statement shall be effective as of a regularly scheduled date and time preceding each monthly meeting.

Additional deposits in the Club account may be made by members in multiples of $10 after the first year of operation.

The Vice President shall appoint at least two partners at each meeting to prepare a report on a security for presentation to the partnership at the following meeting. The Vice President shall remind each person assigned to prepare a report on her or his assignment one week before the meeting.

Buy and/or sell action may be taken after a period of discussion by the members and when voted for by a simple majority of the members' interests.

Approved disbursements must be reconciled with actual disbursements on a monthly basis. All expenses must be pre-approved by a majority vote during the monthly meeting and recorded in the minutes. Following the disbursement, the treasurer is to bring a statement of actual disbursements to the next meeting to be audited for accuracy of payee and amount by two officers. This record should be kept in a notebook maintained by the Secretary.

Sample Partnership Agreement

SAMPLE DOCUMENT: *This is an example of a partnership agreement (or constitution) for an investment club. Your needs may vary, and the governing law may vary from state to state (and country to country). If you want legal advice as to how your investment club's agreement should look, you should consult a licensed attorney.*

Partnership Agreement
of the Raging Fools Investment Club

This AGREEMENT of PARTNERSHIP, effective as of _____ (date) by and between the undersigned:

[*List Names of Club Members*]

NOW, THEREFORE IT IS AGREED:

1. Establishment of Partnership: We, the undersigned Raging Fools [*See the following paragraph*] hereby form a General Partnership in accordance with and subject to the laws of the state of _____ [*State*].

2. Name of Club: The name of the partnership shall be The Raging Fools Investment Club (hereinafter, the "Club") [*If you want another name, that's okay.*]

3. Term: The partnership shall begin on _____ [*date, including year*] and shall continue until December 31 ____ [*same year*] and thereafter from year to year unless earlier terminated as provided hereinafter.

4. Purpose: The only purpose of the partnership is to invest the assets of the partnership solely in stocks, bonds and other securities ("securities") for the education and benefit of the partners.

5. Meetings: Periodic meetings shall be held as determined by the partnership. Snacks may be provided. [*You may specify the frequency of meetings (i.e., monthly) if you want to do so in the document, but that can also be left to the Club's discretion. You don't need to discuss the snacks here.*]

6. Capital Contributions: The partners may make capital contributions to the partnership on the date of each periodic meeting in such amounts as the partnership shall determine, provided, however, that no partner's capital account shall exceed twenty percent (20%) of the sum of the capital accounts of all the partners.

7. Value of the Partnership: The current value of the assets of the partnership, less the current value of the liabilities of the partnership, (hereinafter referred to as the "value of the partnership") shall be determined as of a regularly scheduled date and time ("valuation date") preceding the date of each periodic meeting determined by the Club.

8. Capital Accounts: The Club shall maintain a capital account in the name of each partner. Any increase or decrease in the value of the partnership on any valuation date shall be credited or debited, respectively, to each partner's capital account on that date. Any other method of calculating the value of each partner's capital account may be substituted for this method, provided the substituted method results in exactly the same valuation as previously provided herein. Each partner's contribution to, or capital withdrawal from, the partnership shall be credited, or debited, respectively, to that partner's capital account.

9. Management. Each partner shall participate in the management and conduct of the affairs of the partnership in proportion to his capital account. Except as otherwise determined, all binding business decisions on behalf of the partnership shall be made by the partners whose capital accounts total a majority of the value of the capital accounts of all the partners. [*Alternatively: Each partner shall participate in the management and conduct of the affairs of the partnership equally. Each partner shall have one vote, and all decisions shall be made by a vote of a majority (or supermajority, as specified) vote of all members.*]

10. Sharing of Profits and Losses. Net profits and losses of the partnership shall inure to, and be borne by, the partners, in proportion to the value of each of their capital accounts.

11. Books of Account. The Club shall keep books of account of the transactions of the partnership and they shall at all times be available and open to inspection and examination by any partner.

12. Annual Accounting. A full and complete account of the condition of the partnership shall be made to the partners each calendar year.

13. Bank Account. The partnership may open and maintain a bank account at a bank that the partnership selects. Funds in the bank account

shall be withdrawn by checks signed by any partner designated by the partnership.

14. Brokerage Account. No partner shall be a broker. The partnership may select a broker and enter into such agreements with the broker as required for the purchase or sale of securities. Securities owned by the partnership shall be registered in the partnership name unless the partnership shall designate another name.

Any corporation or transfer agent called upon to transfer any securities to or from the name of the partnership shall be entitled to rely on instructions or assignments signed by any partner without inquiry as to the authority of the person(s) signing such instructions or assignments, or as to the validity of any transfer to or from the name of the partnership.

At the time of a transfer of securities, the corporation or transfer agent is entitled to assume (1) that the partnership is still in existence and (2) that this Agreement is in full force and effect and has not been amended unless the corporation or transfer agent has received written notice to the contrary.

15. No Compensation. No partner shall be compensated for services rendered to the partnership, except reimbursement for expenses undertaken on behalf of the partnership.

16. Additional Partners. Additional partners may be admitted at any time, upon the unanimous consent of the partners, so long as the number of partners does not exceed twenty-five (25).

17. Transfers to a Trust. A partner may, after giving written notice to the other partners, transfer his interest in the partnership to a revocable living trust of which he is the grantor and sole trustee.

18. Removal of a Partner. Any partner may be removed by agreement of the partners whose capital accounts total a majority of the value of all partners' capital accounts. [*Or majority, or supermajority, or unanimously*] Written notice of a meeting where removal of a partner is to be considered shall include a specific reference to this matter. The removal shall become effective upon payment of the value of the removed partner's capital account, which shall be in accordance with the provisions on full withdrawal of a partner noted in paragraphs 20 and 22. The vote action shall be treated as receipt of request for withdrawal.

19. Termination of Partnership. The partnership may be terminated by agreement of the partners whose capital accounts total a majority in value of the capital accounts of all the partners [*or by vote of a majority of the*

members, or by fl vote, or whatever]. Written notice of a meeting where termination of the partnership is to be considered shall include a specific reference to this matter. The partnership shall terminate upon a majority vote of all partners' capital accounts [*or by majority vote, or by fl vote*]. Written notice of the decision to terminate the partnership shall be given to all the partners. Payment shall then be made of all the liabilities of the partnership and a final distribution of the remaining assets either in cash or in kind, shall promptly be made to the partners or their personal representatives in proportion to each partner's capital account.

20. Voluntary Withdrawal of a Partner. Any partner may withdraw a part or all of the value of his capital account in the partnership and the partnership shall continue as a taxable entity.

a) The partner withdrawing a part or all of the value of his capital account shall give notice of such intention in writing to the Secretary. Written notice shall be deemed to be received as of the first meeting of the partnership at which it is presented. If written notice is received between meetings it will be treated as received at the first following meeting.

b) In making payment, the value of the partnership as set forth in the valuation statement prepared for the first meeting following the meeting at which notice is received from a partner requesting a partial or full withdrawal, will be used to determine the value of the partner's account.

c) The partnership shall pay the partner who is withdrawing a portion or all of the value of his capital account in the partnership in accordance with paragraph 22 of this Agreement.

21. Death or Incapacity of a Partner. In the event of the death or incapacity of a partner (or the death or incapacity of the grantor and sole trustee of a revocable living trust, if such trust is partner pursuant to Paragraph 17 hereof), receipt of notice shall be treated as a notice of full withdrawal.

22. Terms of Payment. In the case of a partial withdrawal, payment may be made in cash or securities of the partnership or a mix of each at the option of the partner making the partial withdrawal. In the case of a full withdrawal, payment may be made in cash or securities or a mix of each at the option of the remaining partners. In either case, where securities are to be distributed, the remaining partners select the securities.

a) Where cash is transferred, the partnership shall transfer to the partner (or other appropriate entity) withdrawing a portion or all of his interest in the partnership, an amount equal to the lesser of (i) ninety-seven percent (97%) of the value of the capital account being withdrawn, or (ii) the value of the capital account being withdrawn, less the actual cost to the partnership of selling securities to obtain cash to meet the withdrawal. The amount being withdrawn shall be paid within 10 days after the valuation date used in determining the withdrawal amount.

b) If the partner withdrawing a portion or all of the value of his capital account in the partnership desires an immediate payment in cash, the partnership at its earliest convenience may pay eighty percent (80%) of the estimated value of his capital account and settle the balance in accordance with the valuation and payment procedures set forth in paragraphs 20 and 22.

c) Where securities are transferred, the partnership shall select securities to transfer equal to the value of the capital account or a portion of the capital account being withdrawn (i.e., without a reduction for broker commissions). Securities shall be transferred as of the date of the club's valuation statement prepared to determine the value of that partner's capital account in the partnership. The Club's broker shall be advised that ownership of the securities has been transferred to the partner as of the valuation date used for the withdrawal.

23. Forbidden Acts. No partner shall:

a) Have the right or authority to bind or obligate the partnership to any extent whatsoever with regard to any matter outside the scope of the partnership purpose.

b) Except as provided in paragraph 17, without the unanimous consent of all the other partners, assign, transfer, pledge, mortgage or sell all or part of his interest in the partnership to any other partner or other person whomsoever, or enter into any agreement as the result of which any person or persons not a partner shall become interested with him in the partnership.

c) Purchase an investment for the partnership where less than the full purchase price is paid for same.

d) Use the partnership name, credit or property for other than partnership purposes.

e) Do any act detrimental to the interests of the partnership or which would make it impossible to carry on the business or affairs of the partnership.

f) Under any circumstances offer possible membership rights to any individual or group without the unanimous approval of the partnership.

g)   Forget to bring snacks, when it is his or her turn to bring them.

24. Recognition of Risks. Every investment involves a certain element of risk. By signing this agreement, each partner states that he or she understands and accepts these risks, and understands that no returns are guaranteed.

This Agreement of Partnership shall be binding upon the respective heirs, executors, administrators and personal representatives of the partners.

The partners have caused this Agreement of Partnership to be executed on the dates indicated below, effective as of the date indicated above.

Partners: (Signatures of partners)   Date: _____

SAMPLE

Form **SS-4**

(Rev. December 1995)

Department of the Treasury
Internal Revenue Service

Application for Employer Identification Number

(For use by employers, corporations, partnerships, trusts, estates, churches, government agencies, certain individuals, and others. See instructions.)

▶ Keep a copy for your records.

EIN

OMB No. 1545-0003

Please type or print clearly.

1	Name of applicant (Legal name) (See instructions.)

2	Trade name of business (if different from name on line 1)	3	Executor, trustee, "care of" name

4a	Mailing address (street address) (room, apt., or suite no.)	5a	Business address (if different from address on lines 4a and 4b)

4b	City, state, and ZIP code	5b	City, state, and ZIP code

6	County and state where principal business is located

7	Name of principal officer, general partner, grantor, owner, or trustor—SSN required (See instructions.) ▶

8a Type of entity (Check only one box.) (See instructions.)

☐ Sole proprietor (SSN) _____

☐ Partnership   ☐ Personal service corp.

☐ REMIC   ☐ Limited liability co.

☐ State/local government   ☐ National Guard

☐ Other nonprofit organization (specify) ▶ _____

☐ Other (specify) ▶

☐ Estate (SSN of decedent) _____

☐ Plan administrator-SSN _____

☐ Other corporation (specify) ▶ _____

☐ Trust   ☐ Farmers' cooperative

☐ Federal Government/military ☐ Church or church-controlled organization

(enter GEN if applicable) _____

8b If a corporation, name the state or foreign country (if applicable) where incorporated

State	Foreign country

9 Reason for applying (Check only one box.)

☐ Started new business (specify) ▶ _____

☐ Hired employees

☐ Created a pension plan (specify type) ▶

☐ Banking purpose (specify) ▶ _____

☐ Changed type of organization (specify) ▶ _____

☐ Purchased going business

☐ Created a trust (specify) ▶ _____

☐ Other (specify) ▶

10	Date business started or acquired (Mo., day, year) (See instructions.)	11	Closing month of accounting year (See instructions.)

12 First date wages or annuities were paid or will be paid (Mo., day, year). **Note:** *If applicant is a withholding agent, enter date income will first be paid to nonresident alien. (Mo., day, year)* . . . . ▶

13 Highest number of employees expected in the next 12 months. **Note:** *If the applicant does not expect to have any employees during the period, enter -0-. (See instructions.)* . . . ▶

Nonagricultural	Agricultural	Household

14 Principal activity (See instructions.) ▶

15 Is the principal business activity manufacturing? . . . . ☐ **Yes** ☐ **No**

If "Yes," principal product and raw material used ▶

16 To whom are most of the products or services sold? Please check the appropriate box.

☐ Public (retail)   ☐ Other (specify) ▶

☐ Business (wholesale)

☐ N/A

17a Has the applicant ever applied for an identification number for this or any other business? . . . . ☐ **Yes** ☐ **No**

Note: *If "Yes," please complete lines 17b and 17c.*

17b If you checked "Yes" on line 17a, give applicant's legal name and trade name shown on prior application, if different from line 1 or 2 above.

Legal name ▶   Trade name ▶

17c Approximate date when and city and state where the application was filed. Enter previous employer identification number if known.

Approximate date when filed (Mo., day, year)	City and state where filed	Previous EIN

Under penalties of perjury, I declare that I have examined this application, and to the best of my knowledge and belief, it is true, correct, and complete.

	Business telephone number (include area code)
	Fax telephone number (include area code)

Name and title (Please type or print clearly.) ▶

Signature ▶   Date ▶

Note: *Do not write below this line. For official use only.*

Please leave blank ▶	Geo.	Ind.	Class	Size	Reason for applying

For Paperwork Reduction Act Notice, see page 4.   Cat. No. 16055N   Form **SS-4** (Rev. 12-95)

Boise Street Investment Club
April 9, 1998
Agenda

1. Minutes of previous meeting
2. New Members
3. Sign Agreement
4. Review of ValueLine
5. ValueLine Index
6. Motley Fool Club Info
7. Research for next month
8. Election of officers

Boise St. Investment Club — Minutes of
April 09, 1998 Meeting

- Meeting opened at 7:00 PM. Introductions were made.

- Pam stated that the checks have not been cashed thus far — mix up with Co. had summer helper and so re-submitted.

- Pam discussed that Motley Fool (Co. who has books and publications about investing) has asked her to write and critique article. Congrats!!

- Pam introduced group to ValueLine — look at index further and you will see names of companies in industry that are ranked for timeliness. Go to this to look for a stock you want to research. (i.e., Home building)

- You must always remember things are balanced. You may not always pick the best.

- Column second to last — Est. range of years of appreciation — shows how well their appreciation will be. So, for example: healthcare info. Industry doesn't look so hot.

- Other page out of ValueLine is industry ranking in order of timeliness and it just tells you how they rank overall. Who is going up and down and why.

- Stock eval. Sheet is one Pam made up so that we can look at stock in the same standard manner and evaluate them evenly — comparing apples to apples.

- Look at same industry, similar companies, same data. Then go for it.

So now lets analyze:
1. Name — GAP, Inc
2. Stock Exchange Co. — NYSE
3. Symbol — GPS
4. Source of info. — ValueLine
5. Date: 2-20-98 — date that GAP was analyzed by David (done every 3 mos.)
6. Industry ranking — 9. (least important info.)
7. Timeliness — 1
8. Safety — 3
9. Total debt — 611.2 mill
10. Debt as a percentage of capitalization — 22%
11. Beta — 1.30
12. Sales and earnings — so go back 1 year (1997) — you see 1.34 earning/share.
13. Total sales shares — 6510
    compare these figures

1996 sales — 5284.4	earnings — 1.07
1995 sales — 4395.3	.82
1994 sales — 3722.9	.73
1993 sales — 3295.7	.59

    Comparing each year, looking for a company that's growing their earnings per share at the same rate that they are growing their gross sales. Should be at the same rate.

14. Current Stock price — you should look in the paper as it is more accurate for a daily price. If it is a good buy at $41.00 and now it is $60.00 you should be cautious. You need to make sure the Co. is stable. Is this ratio (P/E) the average for the industry? If not perhaps it is overpriced.

15. If you look at historic P/E ratios and look at the current P/E ratio, you see that GAP's current P/E ratio is higher than the historic average so this looks as though we could be paying too much.

The rest of the form is questions — just answer and you can make a judgement.

- Utility stock — always pay dividends — even if it means borrowing $ they pay dividends in later years. Remember though you always PAY taxes on dividends collected.

- Has gross sales/revenue increased over the last 5 years? The difference on GAP is — gross sales doubled and the revenue increased by more than half so this means this is comparable.

- Pick an industry — please evaluate at least 3 companies for good comparison.

Pat/Robin — office supplies
Marilyn/Carolyn — drug industry
Amy/Kathryn — airline
Marge/Judy — retail stores
Linda/Marlies — environmental
Kelly/Barb — recreation
Margaret/Darlene — manufactured housing

Officer Elections: Any volunteers will be accepted. Think about this please and we will decide.

President — Pam
V.President —
Secretary —
Treasurer —

Next meeting — Second Thursday of month — same time, same place.
Bring $$ for Pizza.
Don't forget your self-addressed stamped envelope.

Thanks

$

Exchange Club
Minutes of April 1, 1998 Meeting

President Pam called the meeting to order at 7:00 p.m. It was held at Nadine's clubhouse, and the following members were present:

Members	Jan	Feb	Mar	Apr	May	June	July	Aug	Sep	Oct	Nov	Dec
Bonita		x	x									
Pam	x	x	x	x								
Peggy	x	x		x								
Marilyn	x	x	x	x								
Madolyn	x	x	x	x								
Sue	x	x	x									
Fran	x											
Nadine	x		x	x								
Patricia	x	x		x								
Cheryl	x	x	x	x								
Jacquie												
Laura	x	x	x	x								
Danean	x	x		x								
Phyllis		x											

I.   Minutes

The minutes of the March 4, 1998 meeting were read.

Action: It was moved, seconded and approved to accept the minutes as read.

II. Treasurer's Report

A. Laura presented the treasurer's report. We currently have a total of $1,634.46 including dividends (but without tonight's contributions) in the broker's account for stock purchases. There is a total of $375.42 in the petty cash account. Petty cash dues of $20 per member are yet to be received from Jacquie and Fran. The total value of our account is $45,308.29.

Action: A motion was made to accept the treasurer's report. This was seconded and approved.

B. NAIC Software Upgrade

Laura reported that the NAIC is offering an upgrade to their soft-ware at a cost of $49. We may have an opportunity to purchase this at the Investors Fair avoiding shipping charges.

Action: Purchase of the software was approved.

III. Stock Reports
A. Updates on Current Holdings

Pam had ValueLines and SSG's on all our holdings. Projected growth was revised downward for Green Tree, Callaway Golf and Applebees. Green Tree has appointed two new directors. The SSG shows this stock to be in the buy range; however, it may be a good time to sell. Further observation is warranted on these three holdings.

AOL split at close-of-business March 16, two for one. We now own 100 shares.

Monaco Coach will split April 16, three for two, effective April 2 for shareholders of record. We will own 150 shares.

Pairgain was the most traded stock on the NASDAQ one day recently.

Marilyn distributed the table of our stocks from the date of purchase and following them through several previous months to the present.

B. Annual Meetings of Current Holdings

Avery Dennison: They were voting for directors, and our members approved those nominated. Madolyn will send in the proxy.

Champion: They too are voting for directors. The members approved those nominated. There is also a proposal to increase the number of common shares to employees for what appears to be stock options or 401k's. This was also approved. Pat will submit our proxy.

Adobe: The members approved their nominees for directors, but did not approve their stock option proposal. Danean will submit the proxy.

Coca Cola: Their nominees for directors were approved, and Pam will send our proxy.

Johnson and Johnson: The nominees for directors were approved. However, their proposal regarding cumulative voting of the direc-tors was not approved. Pam will send in this proxy.

Callaway Golf: The Exchange Club approved their nominees for directors, their stock option plan to increase the company's common stock, and the stock incentive plan. Cheryl will send in this proxy.

C. Stock Purchase

Laura reported we had $2,250 to spend on stock purchase(s). Several stocks were presented for consideration.

Compaq: The ValueLine and SSG were distributed. This stock recently split in January and at close of business 3/31 it was selling for 25 7/8. It is a company on our "ones that got away" list. Their debt is only 1% and the SSG shows them to be in the buy range. Marilyn also stated her broker at Merrill Lynch told her it was on his company's buy list.

Gerber Scientific: This company develops CAD/CAM systems, computer aided design and manufacturing systems. They are 3% in debt, and were selling at 26 1/6 as of 3/31. ValueLine places them above average in their appreciation potential and the SSG shows them to be in the buy range.

Ross Stores: They are 7% in debt, currently selling at 44 and in the buy range.

GAP: They have 22% debt, were selling at 45, and are in the hold range. However, they recently split in December.

Gymboree: This company designs, manufactures and retails high-quality apparel and accessories for children. They were selling for around 27 and were in the buy range. Danean has been very impressed with their products.

Action: A motion was made and seconded to purchase 50 shares of Compaq. This was approved.

IV. Investors' Fair April 18

Everyone was reminded of the local chapter's Portland-Northwest Investors Fair on April 18 being held at the Double Tree Hotel-Columbia River (formerly Red Lion Inn). Registration is $40 at the door.

V. New Business:

None.

VI.   Announcements:

Pam has written a handout "Stock Market Fundamentals." If you are interested in receiving a copy, give Pam a call.

VII. Next Meeting:

The next meeting is scheduled for Wednesday, May 6 at Nadine's clubhouse. Dinner will be at the Acapulco Restaurant just east of Mall 205 on Washington, 5:30 p.m.

There being no further business, the meeting adjourned at 9:00 p.m.

Recorded by:

Marilyn, Secretary

HERA INVESTMENT GROUP
There is a little Hera in all of us
August 6, 1997

PRESENT		**ABSENT**
Dana	Susan	
Linda	Debbie	Sandy
Angie	Amy	Kari
Donna	Julie	Nancy
Jackie	Kris	Sharon
Vickie		

Meeting was called to order by Julie.

We welcomed our guests: Marie   Erika   ; Sheila   ; Debi   ; Dody   '; Virginia
        We listed highlights of the club.

The minutes were read.

Motion made by Susan to accept the minutes as read.
Seconded by Vickie.
Motion passed

Financial report was given by Dana. We have $474.00 in our money market. The net market value of our stocks as of 08/05/97 was $17,178.00. We have 1223.67 in our checking account. A grand total of $18,875.67 and this does not include the dues collected tonight.

Motion made by Donna to accept the financial report as read.
Seconded by Jackie
Motion passed

We discussed putting together an article about our club for Better Investing. Julie will write something so we can have it on file to mail.

Motion made by Susan to sell all McDonald's stock
Seconded by Angie
Motion passed

Amy will give reports on some other fast food chains to see if there is another we may want to purchase. Wendy's, White Castle, Burger King, or Starbucks.

Value Lines and reports were given by Angie, Linda and Donna on Harsco Corp and Albertson.

We established a Nominating Committee of three members, Jackie, Vickie, & Angie.

The guest were then encouraged to ask questions and the Club answered them.

The September meeting will be held September 3rd at the Dublin Library 7p.m..

The meeting was adjourned.
Motion made by Jackie
Seconded by Vickie
Motion passed

Hera Investment Group - *AGENDA*

Regular Monthly Meeting   **August 6,** 1997 - 7:00 pm
at Dublin Library - DUBLIN

✓ a: Welcome Visitors (= DoDi S, MARi .., Virginia R.)
✓ b: 50/50 Raffle ($ 14⁰⁰ =club
✓ c: Collection of monthly dues

*   *   *   * **7:00 PM** *   *   *   *   *   *

1- Call meeting to order

2- Recording Partner: Minutes of last meeting
* Corrections or additions to minutes
* Motion to accept minutes , as printed/read (or corrected)

3- Financial Partner's Report $ 1223.67 (check. acct bal before tonight)
   $ 474.00 (money market account)
   $ 17,178.00 (portfolio value) = TOTAL : $ 18,875.67

Reporter	Stock	Shares	Notes:
Dana	* Status of: Boeing	(20 shares)	
Sandy	* Status of : Meditronic	(15 shares)	
Nancy	* Status of: Fed Nat Mortgage	(20 shares	
Amy	* Status of: McDonald's	(10 shares)	
Angie	* Status of: Diebold	(70 shares)	
Julie	* Status of: Intel Corp	(20 shares	
Dana	* Status of: Harley Davidson	(20 shares)	
Susan	* Status of: Hewlett Packard	(25 shares)	
Donna	* Status of: Emerson Electric	(10 shares)	

Old Business:

1- Do we want to submit Club article to Better Investing Magazine?? < Yes- Julie will do rough draft.

2- What do we want to do with our McDonald's stock (10 shares = $500)? < Sell All 10 shares

3- ⌒

New Business:

1- Any new stock recommendations? (Southwest Airlines, C-Cube, Worthington Industries) ???
Should we purchase any additional shares of current stocks in portfolio ????? —(yes, see below)

2- Establish Nominating Committee > Linda, Angie, Jackie

3- other: Buy 10 sh. Albertsons   + Buy 15 sh. Pfizer

4- other: > set up workshop For Next MTg - "How To Read The Value Line Page"

Next Meeting: Date: **September , 2nd - Wednesday** Time: 7:00 PM
Place: **Hilliard Library**

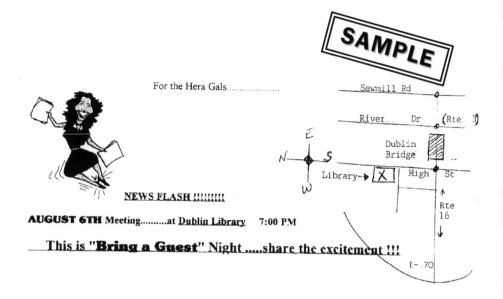

For the Hera Gals....................

NEWS FLASH !!!!!!!!!

AUGUST 6TH Meeting..........at Dublin Library   7:00 PM

This is "**Bring a Guest**" Night .....share the excitement !!!

HAVE YOU BEEN WATCHING THE STOCK MARKET LATELY ???   YAHOOOOO !!!!!
If not, you're in for a surprise ....our research is really paying off in the strong stocks we've selected and **THIS IS ONLY THE BEGINNING!** ..look at the enclosed E-Trade reports.....and SMILE !

Now, on to club business:

1-   Invite a friend to our meeting ..... **Earn Points !!**
       (we prefer they visit at least 2 meetings to get a "taste" of what we are and what we do.....)

2-   A few of us will bring "refreshments", so if others could bring cold cans of drinks
       or cookies, this would be helpful......let's make our guests feel welcome.

3-   NAIC dues are due this meeting so make your check for $49.00 ($35 + $14)
       If you can't attend, send your check and dues with another member or mail it to me..... we
       should not be using "investment money" to cover someone's dues expense .....please be
       responsible for yourself. I will be sending in total NAIC dues payment on August 10th.

4-   If you are presenting a stock at the meeting, please make extra packets so that our guests
       can actually see what goes into selecting an investment. Be sure to provide all the required
       research: 2 articles, _____ a Value-Line Report. _____ a Standard -Poor Report.
                     a value-line summary   and _____ current price.
       This gives the rest of the group valuable information for making a decision.

5-   Intel split !!!!!!!! on July 14th.....our 20 shares turned into 40 shares....(see E-Trade reports
       attached) and its price is growing AGAIN!!!
       Medtronic is due to split Sept 23rd........ !!

6-   Yes, we are having a Value Line Workshop NEXT MONTH (September Meeting) .
       Please make a point of attending.......you're cheating yourself if you don't...
       .(your guests are invited too) At Dublin Library again......Sept. 3rd ! Wednesday 7:00 PM
       Next month's News Flash will list items to bring , etc......

See you at the meeting.   *Dana*

       PS: Again, congratulations to us all for having the "guts" to form this group and for making it
       fun and successful.   HERA would be proud of us !

YOU'RE INVITED !!!!!

by _Dana_
TO

HERA INVESTMENT GROUP

VISITOR'S EVENING
(light refreshments will be served)

Date: **Wednesday, August 6th**
Time: **7:00 PM**
Place: **Dublin Library** -Meeting Room

Did you know??????

*We've just celebrated our 2nd year as an Investment Club.

*We're proud to say our portfolio is worth **over $17,000.** (WOW!!!!!)

*Our membership consists of 16 women, each contributing $35.00 each month.

 *Our ages range from 24 to 60-plus. We're looking for "long-term members", so
    we require visitors to attend a minimum 2 meetings before committing to
    a membership. Each member is expected to contribute to discussion, research,
    plus serve on one of the various committees.
    (We all started out knowing VERY LITTLE.....but we learn something at each
    meeting.....we often use the "buddy system" for research and projects.)

*By educating ourselves, we've learned how to research data to find those companies
    who show a successful future...a future we want to be a part of ..... Some of the
    companies currently being researched: Nike, Reebok, Coca Cola, C-Cube,
    Southwest Airlines, Nextel Communications, Airtouch, Worthington Industries,
    KeyBank, BancOne............(which one(s) will get OUR MONEY ?????????)

*Our portfolio currently consists of these companies:

McDonald's	**Fanny Mae**	**Diebold**	**Hewlett Packard**
Intel	**Harley Davidson**	**Boeing**	**General Electric**
Medtronic	**Emerson Electric**